CANCELLED

D1365789

You and Your Small Wonder

Other Works by Merle B. Karnes

Early Childhood Enrichment Series
GOAL
    Language Development
    Mathematical Concepts
    Beginning Science
    Beginning Health and Nutrition
Karnes Early Language Activities (GEM)
Learning Language at Home
Creative Games for Learning
Creative Art for Learning
Learning Mathematics Concepts at Home
Small Wonder!
    Level 1: Activities for Baby's First 18 Months
    Level 2: Activities for Toddlers 18-36 Months
You and Your Small Wonder: Activities for
    Busy Parents and Babies

You and Your Small Wonder

Activities for Parents and Toddlers on the Go

Merle B. Karnes

AGS ®
American Guidance Service
Circle Pines, Minnesota 55014

AGS staff participating in the development and production of this publication:

Program Development

Dorothy Chapman, Director
James Wendorf, Senior Coordinating Editor
Marjorie Lisovskis, Assistant Editor

Product Development

David Youngquist, Director
Lynn Rusch, Materials Development Manager
Carol Wagner, Production Manager
Maureen Wilson, Art Director
Sylvia Carsen, Production Artist

Photographs:

Niedorf Photography

Library of Congress Catalog Card Number: 82-71049
ISBN 0-913476-59-5

Once again, to Gregory and Sheri,
the wonderful parents of my grandson, Joshua,
who is indeed a "small wonder."

Contents

Acknowledgments

Book 2 of *You and Your Small Wonder* is a handbook of activities that complements Level 2 of the *Small Wonder* program. It culminates many years of experience working with parents of toddlers and with toddlers themselves. I especially wish to thank the dozens of parents and children who inspired the book. Their valuable contributions have been incorporated in the activities.

I am indebted to Paula Strong and Barbara Franke, early childhood specialists and themselves mothers of toddlers, who made major contributions to the writing and field testing of the activities.

I wish to thank Susan S. Aronson, M.D., F.A.A.P., for carefully reviewing the activities for health and safety concerns. Thanks also to Susanne P. Miskiewicz, mother and reading specialist, and to Diane Stanford, Director of the Ashland Child Development Center, for reviewing the manuscript and offering valuable suggestions.

I extend my appreciation to the entire staff of AGS for the knowledge, creativity, skills, and encouragement they provided. My thanks to Don Michaelis and his marketing staff for their research endorsing the need for this book, to Maureen Wilson for the page design, and to Carol Wagner for coordinating production. To James Wendorf I am particularly grateful. His meticulous editing of the manuscript and his attention to its format have enhanced the quality of the book. I am likewise appreciative of the encouragement and creative ideas provided by Dorothy Chapman, Director of Program Development. Last but not least, to John Yackel, President of AGS, I express my gratitude for supporting the development of *You and Your Small Wonder*.

Merle B. Karnes, Ed.D.
Professor of Education
Institute for Child Behavior and Development
University of Illinois, Urbana

Introduction

The toddler months are guaranteed to be packed with action. Your child is growing and changing at a rapid rate: He's* beginning to understand language and use it to communicate thoughts and feelings — even if he is saying only a handful of words, he probably understands much of what you say to him. He is able to solve more and more problems that he encounters in his everyday world. Undressing a doll and matching lids to pans require concentrated thought and physical coordination! Your child is also mastering many physical skills such as climbing, running, and jumping. And during the toddler months he is starting to play alongside and cooperate with other children. This is also an age of burgeoning independence — a favorite phrase for many toddlers is "Me do."

Book 2 of *You and Your Small Wonder* can prepare you for the exciting and challenging months ahead. It is designed to help you encourage your child as he develops during the toddler months. The activities cover physical, emotional, and intellectual growth as well as language development in children between 18 and 36 months of age. They are based on activities featured in the *Small Wonder* kit, which was carefully field tested in homes, centers, and clinics across the United States.** Like all parents, you'd like to know whether your child is progressing normally and whether you're doing the best you can to encourage him. The information on child development presented in the following pages will help assure you. In addition, the activities will enhance your own special ways of playing with your toddler and teaching him.

Some activities will undoubtedly give you new ideas; others will reinforce what you're already doing with your toddler. Because your day is very busy, many of the activities are designed to fit into your everyday schedule. Others are for special moments that you set aside to spend with your little one. All the activities give your child a chance to learn in a playful atmosphere. They also give you the opportunity to share the formative experiences of your toddler's life and to become a better observer of his development.

Reading a picture book.

---

*The opening sections of *You and Your Small Wonder* alternate in the use of masculine and feminine pronouns. The information presented here applies to boys and girls alike.

**Merle B. Karnes, *Small Wonder! Level 2: Activities for Toddlers 18-36 Months* (Circle Pines, Minn.: American Guidance Service, 1981). For information about the complete kit, turn to the section entitled *More About Small Wonder*.

Introduction

HOW TO USE THE ACTIVITIES

The *Small Wonder* activities are grouped into nine thematic units. These units feature activities that can be done at a particular time (for example, *Chore-time Chums*), or in a special place (for example, *Growing with the Grass*), or with certain people (for example, *Teaching — Family Style*). Within a unit there are 16-18 activities arranged by age range: each unit has several activities for toddlers 18-24 months, 24-30 months, and 30-36 months. If you're looking for something new to do at bathtime with your 20-month-old, all you have to do is turn to the activities for 18-24 month olds in *Bathtime Business*.

As you use the *Small Wonder* activities with your child, let the time you spend be relaxing. You will not only be enhancing his normal development, but also strengthening the bond between you. To get the most out of the activities, keep in mind the following suggestions:

- Choose activities that are in your child's developmental range. You have already discovered what a unique person your child is — make sure you give him a chance to develop in his own way and at his own pace. He may master some tasks before the normal age, and he may be a bit slower with others. You may want to start with the more challenging activities in the age range *below* that of your child. For example, if he is 26 months old, choose activities in the 18-24 month range. When he masters those activities, go on to his own age range. (If your toddler is 18-24 months old, you may want to use activities for 15-18 month olds in Book 1 of *You and Your Small Wonder*.)

- Some activities are not limited to one age range, especially storytelling, songs and rhymes, bathtub games, and outdoor activities. As your toddler develops and does these activities over and over, he will expand on them — so don't put away his favorites once he masters them.

- Your toddler may perform certain activities very well. If so, go on to the next age range and choose similar types of activities. (The index of activities at the back of this book will help you choose.) But be careful not to pressure him to try activities that are beyond his ability — he will probably become discouraged and lose interest. Continue more advanced activities only if your child seems to be enjoying the challenge.

- Become familiar with an activity before you begin. After reading it, gather all the materials required. Although you and your toddler should feel free to change the activity to suit your own interests and needs, you will enjoy yourselves more if you know what the activity calls for.

- Repeat the activity. The first time you present an activity, it may seem too difficult for your child. Try it two or three times before deciding that it's too hard. Don't frustrate your toddler by encouraging him to do something he can't do. But keep in mind that he will complete many of the tasks only after he does them several times — how many times depends on the difficulty of the skill and your child's unique rate of learning.

Even when your toddler seems to have learned a skill, he may forget it. He may be concentrating on a new skill, or he may have learned the skill only for the moment. Skills and abilities will become permanent as your child does them over and over. Once he masters a task, he will still enjoy doing it again and again. The success he enjoys at one activity may motivate him to try another.

Before you put aside a particular activity because it seems too easy or too difficult, ask yourself the following questions: Can my child do the activity easily? If so, does he still enjoy doing the activity or does it bore him? Does the activity seem to frustrate him because it's too hard?

Learning to take turns.

TEACHING TIPS AND GUIDELINES

You have much to offer your toddler! Use your imagination to add special touches to an activity, or to expand and vary it. Rely on your own unique abilities and interests — whether they be musical, artistic, athletic, or other abilities — to make learning an enjoyable experience for your child. Your enthusiasm, your approach to an activity, and your willingness to try new approaches will affect your toddler's level of achievement and the way he feels about himself.

Keep in mind the following teaching tips while using the *Small Wonder* activities. They have helped other mothers, fathers, and caregivers. If your child has older brothers or sisters, you may want to stress these tips to them so that they learn how to play with the little one in the family.

Choose the right time for the activity.
- Your child needs to be attentive, so don't attempt an activity when he is fussy, sleepy, or distracted.
- Respect your toddler's feelings. Don't take him away from another activity he is enjoying to work on the activity of your choice.
- Work for short periods (5-10 minutes).
- Very gradually increase the time your child works on an activity.

Fit the activity to your child's mood.
- "Sit-down" tasks and story time are good choices when your toddler is quiet or physically tired but alert.
- If he is in an active mood, choose an activity that stresses physical skills.

Set the stage for learning.
- Be prepared by gathering all materials beforehand.
- Eliminate as many distractions as possible. Put away other toys, turn off the TV or radio, and try to occupy other children with different activities or include them directly in the toddler's activity.
- Provide safe, comfortable surroundings: low tables, booster seats, adequate lighting, and plenty of space for movement.
- Be enthusiastic! If you come to the activity with energy and interest, your toddler will be more responsive.

Praise your toddler's efforts as well as his successes.
- A pat, a hug, a smile, or a kiss is an encouraging sign that your young child will understand.
- Praise your toddler immediately after he succeeds or makes a good effort. Young children learn to do things most quickly when praise is given promptly. They need to know when they are on the right track, since they learn so many things by trial and error.

- Give positive but realistic praise for your child's efforts. If he tries to throw a ball to you but misses by a yard, it isn't encouraging to say, "That was terrific!" Such praise is meaningless, and it could actually discourage him. Say instead, "That was a good try! Try again."
- Physical punishment and verbal criticism discourage learning.
- A disapproving or disappointed tone of voice often speaks more harshly to a toddler than your actual words. Remember that what you say and how you say it can build your child's self-confidence or destroy it.

Keep up with your toddler!
- Sometimes a young toddler's hands are quicker than your eye. Your child will want to manipulate the materials you show him, but not always in the way you intend. Give him time to play as he wishes with the materials. Then, when you think the time is right, introduce the activity you want to work on.

Be sure your child understands your directions.
- Your toddler may not be able to do a task because he doesn't understand what you are asking him to do. Repeat your directions several ways to be sure he understands.
- You may also want to demonstrate. By watching you, your toddler learns what you are asking or saying.

Be flexible in your approach.
- Toddlers can be stubborn and willful! Your child may choose not to do an activity simply to oppose you — it's a way of testing his own independence. If your approach is positive, he may want to participate in spite of himself.
- Learn how to spark your child's curiosity during planned activities. He may approach new tasks cautiously, or

he may plunge right into a challenge. He may like to explore things alone and work by himself, or he may enjoy some company while he learns. Adjust your ways of presenting activities to match your toddler's personality and mood.

HOW TO INCLUDE OLDER BROTHERS AND SISTERS IN SMALL WONDER ACTIVITIES

If your toddler has older siblings, you know that brothers and sisters don't always get along. Despite your best efforts, jealousies are very likely to exist. Older children can be impatient with a younger sibling. After all, he might interfere in their games and mess up their play area. But there are probably other times when older brothers and sisters adore the toddler in the family and play well with him. However they feel about the toddler, you can use *Small Wonder* activities to help brothers and sisters become involved with him and include him as a valued member of the family.

When you are doing a *Small Wonder* activity, involve your other child or children in some way, if they seem interested. Depending on age, he or she might assist you or take part in the activity along with the toddler. For example, if you are teaching the toddler to walk up stairs, an older child might walk with him or say a rhyme with you to encourage the toddler as he goes up alone. If your toddler is working a puzzle, you can provide more difficult ones for older children and comment on their own attempts to work their puzzles. The section entitled *Teaching — Family Style* suggests specific activities you can do with the entire family.

Health and Safety

NUTRITION

Nutrition is a very popular and controversial topic these days. "Health foods" are becoming more and more popular and the word *natural* is used to describe everything from potato chips to ice cream. It can all be very confusing. Yet there are some basics of nutrition that can help you choose foods and plan meals to ensure that your toddler has a healthy and balanced diet.

The Basics of Nutrition
Although *calories* may be a dirty word to you, your toddler needs calories to grow and stay healthy. The term *calorie* refers to the energy-producing value in foods. Everything she* does — exercise, play, sleep, and even eat — requires calories, but the amount of calories needed varies from child to child and from time to time with the same child. Sometime during the toddler months, your child's growth will slow down and so she will require fewer calories in her diet. She is probably a good judge of how much she *needs* to eat — she will stop when she is full. Don't urge her to "clean her plate"; doing so may only help to make her fat. And don't offer her lots of sweets, which are hard for anyone to resist. The calories your child needs should come from a balance of the basic foods: proteins, starches, sugars, and fats.

Proteins. Your child's body uses proteins to build body tissue, especially muscles. To grow normally, her body needs *complete* proteins — proteins that contain the eight essential amino acids. Meat, fish, eggs, soybeans, and milk all contain complete proteins. You can combine other foods to form complete proteins — for example, grains (bread, cereal, rice) and legumes (peanuts, beans, peas). Such combinations

*The opening sections of *You and Your Small Wonder* alternate in the use of feminine and masculine pronouns. The information presented here applies to girls and boys alike.

are contained in bean tacos, peanut-butter sandwiches, and casseroles such as rice with peas. When you combine grains or legumes with even small amounts of milk, cheese, or meat, the total protein quality is improved. Such dishes include oatmeal with milk, cheese and noodles, and chicken-and-rice casseroles. Even on a limited budget you can provide your child and the rest of your family with low-cost meals that are high in protein.

Carbohydrates. Carbohydrates provide the body with starches and sugars — the quick-energy foods. Carbohydrates are obtained from grains and tuberous vegetables (potatoes, beets, carrots, turnips, radishes). Grains and tubers also provide the body with roughage to help in digestion.

Fats. Your toddler's body uses fats to support and protect her vital organs and to insulate her body from cold. Since fats are digested slowly, they also add staying power to foods; your toddler doesn't feel hungry soon after a meal. However, children can't digest fats as well as adults, so don't feed your little one too many fatty foods. Milk fat, egg yolk, butter, margarine or peanut butter used as a spread on bread, and fish oils provide adequate fats.

Vitamins and minerals. Vitamins and minerals are the body's protectors. They keep the body tissues healthy and help the organs function normally. The body receives many vitamins and minerals from fruits and vegetables. Proteins, milk, and carbohydrates provide other vitamins and minerals.

Milk. Although your child's requirements of protein, most vitamins, and iron are less than an adult's, her growing body needs more minerals, calcium, phosphorus, and vitamin D. Fortified whole or skim milk provides all of these latter nutrients.

Snacks

A toddler usually cannot eat enough at one meal to last her until the next. A cranky, crying toddler might need nothing more than a nutritious mid-morning, mid-afternoon, or evening snack to recharge her.

Sugary or starchy snacks start to be digested right away in your child's mouth, from enzymes in her saliva. These foods are absorbed into the body quickly and give "quick" energy. But this energy is quickly used up and so it doesn't last long. Protein adds "staying power." If you include some protein at snacktime, snack energy will last a lot longer.

Snack foods can be tasty *and* high in food value. Try some of the following combinations of foods: crackers with small pieces of cheese or meat; fresh fruit with some cheese; bland pudding, fruit puddings, or custard; a glass of milk with peanut butter on crackers or with a peanut-butter or oatmeal cookie. Such snacks as these can provide quick energy and some staying power — enough to last until mealtime.

Behavior at Mealtime

If your toddler is a picky eater, you may dread mealtime. You may be concerned that she isn't eating enough or that she isn't eating a balanced diet. To ensure that your toddler gets adequate nutrition, offer small servings of several foods and urge her to eat at least some of each. Then give her more of her favorites.

Whatever you do, try not to let mealtime become a battle of wits between you and your child. Stay calm. If you fuss over how much she eats or what she eats, she might learn to use mealtime as a way to get attention or gain control over you.

Never use food as a reward for good behavior; nor should you deny your child food because of inappropriate behavior.

Doing what you do!

Food is food. If you use it for any other purpose, you are only asking for trouble at mealtime.

Try to make eating time a happy time. Your child will enjoy using a straw to drink with or drinking from a cup with a favorite television or storybook character on it. You might use party napkins sometimes, or make a construction-paper placemat with her picture on it. To avoid unnecessary restlessness at the table, remove distractions: turn off the television, keep toys off the table, and keep desserts out of sight until the end of the meal.

Remember that while your child is young, you are helping her develop tastes and eating habits that will probably stay with her for life. If you encourage her to eat balanced meals and nutritious foods, you are doing her and her body a big favor.

SAFETY IN YOUR HOME

You have already lived through the months when anything even remotely hazardous must be out of the baby's reach. By now your child has learned a lot about the dangers in her world — both from experience and from your warnings. But an active and curious toddler can get herself into lots of dangerous trouble, so you still should be careful about the potential hazards in your home.

Some safety considerations are obvious, such as the quality of toys, the condition of play areas, and the storage of tools, equipment, and hazardous substances. Other considerations are less obvious, such as the condition of household furnishings and the presence of subtle dangers around the house. Keep in mind that toddlers have a very high accident rate.

Accidents happen in even the safest households, so be prepared for emergencies. Keep important phone numbers listed near each telephone in your house. List the numbers of your child's doctor, a nearby hospital, a poison control center, an ambulance service, as well as the police and fire departments. When you have a sitter in your home, show that person the list of numbers and write down where you can be reached.

Toys

Choose toys made of such sturdy, nontoxic materials as wood, metal, or high-impact plastic. Avoid toys with small parts (less than 1" diameter) that can easily be broken off. Check for low flammability on stuffed and fabric toys. Don't buy your child missiles or toy guns that actually discharge an object. These may cause eye, ear, or other injuries. Teach your toddler not to poke pointed objects (crayons, scissors, sticks) into her own or anyone else's ears — they may puncture an eardrum.

For additional information on safety standards for toys and clothing, write to the United States Consumer Product Safety Commission, Washington, D.C. 20207.

Play Areas

- Check the floor of all play areas for electrical cords on lamps and small appliances. Children can trip over cords, pulling heavy objects onto the floor or themselves.
- Plug unused electrical outlets with protective safety caps, and teach your toddler not to play with outlets.
- Make sure you have no poisonous houseplants. (See the section in this guide entitled *Poisonous Plants*.)
- Check tables for sturdiness (even child-size furniture can be unsteady).
- Windows that children can reach should have locks and a restraining bar or adjustable safety catches that can be locked open at a safe width of 4". Teach your toddler not to sit on window ledges.
- Make sure that only lead-free paint is used for painted surfaces in the play area, as well as other areas of your home.
- Store toys on sturdy shelves or bookcases that won't fall over onto your child. If a bookcase is tall and unsteady, anchor it to the wall.
- A toy chest with a heavy lid should have a catch to hold the box lid open without falling and thereby pinching fingers or hitting a child's head.

In the Kitchen

- Always turn pot handles away from the stove edge so they will be out of your child's reach.
- Do not let your toddler climb onto the stove or the oven door — she could manipulate the knobs and turn on the gas or electricity.
- Keep matches out of reach.
- Cupboards and drawers containing knives or dangerous or breakable kitchen equipment should have childproof secondary latches. Those devices are readily available at hardware stores and are easily installed.
- Install safety catches on all drawers so your child cannot pull them all the way out.

- Keep cleaning supplies out of your toddler's reach in an overhead cupboard or in a cupboard fitted with a safety latch. Never keep cleaning agents, waxes, salves, disinfectants, dyes, or bleaches under the sink.
- Always leave labels on containers. Clearly label containers if you transfer something into them for convenience.

In the Bathroom

Your bathroom is probably filled with poisons. These poisons don't look poisonous because they are usually in the form of medication.

- For safety's sake, use childproof safety latches on medicine cabinets and vanity drawers.
- Never leave medicines or vitamins within a child's reach.
- Avoid taking medications in front of children.
- Throw away unused prescriptions.
- Never give medicine in the dark — you might accidentally give the wrong one.
- Use a rubber mat or appliques on the bottom of the tub to prevent accidental slipping. Grab bars will provide extra safety.
- Mark hot and cold taps clearly.
- To prevent scalds in the tub, run cold water before hot and then run some cold water to cool off metal fixtures. Set your water heater at 120° F just in case your child turns on the hot water by herself.
- Put away small electrical appliances like hair dryers, sunlamps, shavers, and electric toothbrushes as soon as you're finished with them.

Stairways

- Accompany your toddler when she climbs up or down open risers, which are often found in basements. A small child could slip between the risers.
- Openings below a handrail should be blocked by a solid panel or by balusters so that your child can't climb or slip through.
- Arrange balusters vertically to discourage climbing. Space them only 3 1/2" apart so her head will not get wedged between them.
- Make sure that handrails are secure. Never allow a child to slide down handrails — she could fall off on the way down or land very hard when she gets to the bottom.

Storage Areas

- Maintenance equipment, such as hedge trimmers, mowers, and rakes, should be kept away from young children, preferably in locked cabinets or rooms.
- Hand tools and power tools should also be stored out of reach, in a locked place. When using power tools, never leave them running if your toddler is nearby.
- Safely store gas cans, fertilizers, herbicides, plant food, rat or rodent killers, kerosene, laundry aids, and oils. Take extra precautions when using them near children of any age.
- Make sure that doors on closets have knobs on both sides so that your toddler will not be trapped inside.

Outdoors

- If possible, choose a play area for your toddler that is away from a street or parking area. A play area adjoining a street should have guard rails, a fence, or other barriers.
- Make sure you can see the play area clearly. Toddlers need to be watched during outdoor play to avoid accidents and to prevent them from wandering away.
- Check the grounds for broken glass, pop tops, rusted metal objects, and other hazards — especially if your child will be going barefoot.
- Choose a play area that is partially shaded during the day, or take other

Learning to draw a straight line.

precautions against a hot summer sun (for example, sun hats, sun-screen lotion).

- Choose toys for use outdoors that are appropriate to the child's age. A scooter, for example, should fit the size of the child who rides it. It can be dangerous to choose a toy that your toddler will "grow into."
- Keep in mind that loose or long clothing can get caught in spokes and wheels.
- Do not leave a wading pool filled with water that is uncovered.
- Let the sun and rain purify sandboxes; don't cover them with sheets of plastic or canvas. A cover of wire netting or window screening will let in air and keep out animals.
- Make sure that wooden equipment is splinter-free and has rounded edges to prevent injuries.
- Heavy play equipment should be sunk in concrete deep enough so that it won't pull out of the ground.
- Check equipment for nontoxic finishes and for sturdiness. Now and then, check for sharp edges, loose parts, and rusted areas.
- Sand or grass under slides and other equipment will cushion a fall.

- Teach your child not to push and shove on play equipment.
- Maintain equipment each season to ensure safety.

POISONOUS PLANTS

Plants are beautiful, but they may be harmful to your child if she eats any part of them. Some house and garden plants are fatal. As a general rule, keep houseplants out of your toddler's reach and check to see if any plants in or around her outdoor play area are poisonous.

Garden plants that have fatal effects include castor beans, laurels, rhododendron, azaleas, and the berries from daphne plants, yew plants, and mistletoe. Wild plants that may cause death include nightshade and hemlock plants, and the berries from moonseed plants. Houseplants that cause fatalities include the seeds of rosary peas and the leaves from poinsettias.

Household plants with poisonous effects include the dieffenbachia and elephant ears.

Some parts of fruit and vegetable plants are poisonous — the leaves of rhubarbs, the foliage and vine of both tomato and potato plants, the twigs of cherry trees, and the leaves of peach trees.

Several types of shade trees have poisonous parts — the acorns and foliage of oak trees; the shoots, leaves, and bark of elderberry and black walnut trees; and the seedpods from golden chain trees.

Many beautiful flowering plants have poisonous parts — the bulbs of hyacinths, narcissus, and daffodils; the leaves and branches of oleanders; the leaves of foxgloves; the young plants and seeds of larkspurs; the leaves of lily-of-the-valley; all parts of the buttercup and the jack-in-the-pulpit.

If your child eats a poisonous plant, induce vomiting and obtain medical treatment immediately. For more information about dangerous plants, contact the poison control center in your area.

A WORD ABOUT CHILD ABUSE AND NEGLECT

Your child is a marvel, and you love her very much. But the toddler months can cause extra strain for parents and other members of the family. Toddlers can be very stubborn and emotionally demanding. Toddlerhood is often an age of tantrums and rigid behavior. At these stressful times, some adults respond with abusive behavior.

A growing number of people are seeing that child abuse is a more widespread problem than they had thought. Although child abuse and neglect are not normal, they affect normal people in all walks of life. A person does not have to be mentally ill to be a child abuser.

In addition to physical abuse, parents can neglect their children by not giving them the love and attention they need or by failing to feed and clothe them properly. Sexual abuse of children is widespread.

Potential abusers include people who were themselves emotionally neglected or physically abused as children, people under severe stress, and people who lack a sense of their own worth. People who are dependent on alcohol or drugs run a higher risk of neglecting or abusing their children than those who are not. Ignorance can create the conditions for child abuse — ignorance of the way a child develops or of the special needs of a handicapped child.

If you are worried that you might abuse or neglect your toddler — in any of the ways just described — talk with someone who understands. Call your county's Public Health Nursing Services or Department of Social Services for help. For further information, write to Parents Anonymous, an organization whose sole purpose is to help parents who have abused or neglected their children or who fear they might. The national address is 22330 Hawthorne Blvd. #208, Torrance, CA 90505. Phone (213) 371-3501.

Milestones of Development

Between 18 and 36 months, toddlers develop at greatly varying rates. One 20-month-old may talk in short sentences while another uses only single words. One child may put together five-piece puzzles at 24 months while another does not accomplish this feat until 30 months. The following milestones indicate some skills and behaviors that are developed during the toddler months. They are *approximate*, and so shouldn't be seen as a rigid schedule of development. Because there is so much variation among children, the milestones are presented in three-month intervals for toddlers between 18 and 24 months and in six-month intervals for toddlers between 24 and 36 months.

18-21 Months
- Runs without falling.
- Walks up and down stairs with adult help.
- Walks backwards and sideways.
- Jumps in place one time.
- Kicks large ball.
- Throws small ball.
- Shows hand preference.
- Makes circular scribbles.
- Holds two objects in one hand.
- Strings large beads.
- Unzips zipper.
- Washes and dries hands with assistance.
- Feeds himself.
- Removes own clothes.
- Imitates adults, copies their activities, and enjoys dress-up in adult clothes.
- Does not share own possessions.
- Plays alongside other children, not with them; but does enjoy interactive games such as tag and ring-around-the-rosie.
- Enjoys rhythm — rocking, swinging on swings, dancing to music.
- Uses one- or two-word phrases to make requests: "Cup," "Go up."
- Asks, "What's that?"
- Identifies familiar objects and pictures in books.

21-24 Months
- Jumps off low elevations (box, bottom stair, short stool).
- Pedals small tricycle.
- Throws ball into basket.
- Completes puzzle of two or three pieces.
- Unwraps packages and candy wrappers; peels bananas.
- Turns pages one at a time.
- Zips jacket zipper.
- Uses cup without spilling much.
- Helps dress himself.
- Enjoys listening to stories and looking at books.
- Enjoys playing in and with water.
- Enjoys sound repetition (lyrics, singsongs, nursery rhymes).

Spooning improves eye-hand coordination.

- Is very sensitive to criticism.
- Uses the words *mine, me, you,* and *I* — often incorrectly.

24-30 Months
- Walks on tiptoe.
- Walks up and down stairs, holding on to rail.
- Can unscrew jar lids.
- Can move each finger separately.
- Builds tower of six or seven small blocks.
- Imitates circular strokes with a pencil.
- Matches identical objects.
- Tries to be independent: "Me do it!"
- Plays in company of other children, but not with them.
- Echoes adult speech. For example, if adult says, "Put the pail away," he might say, "Put pail away."
- Asks "where" questions: "Where ball?"
- Uses plurals: "cookies," "dogs," "foots."
- Distinguishes between *one* and *many*. For example, he might call one ball "a ball" and several balls "two balls."
- Is becoming aware of opposites: *yes/no, fast/slow, up/down*.
- Uses phrases or sentences of three or more words.
- Understands between 300 and 1000 words.

30-36 Months
- Jumps up and down several times.
- Steps over low obstacles.
- Modulates body by changing speed or direction, dodging obstacles, turning corners.
- Catches large ball with both arms extended.
- Builds tower of eight or more small blocks.
- Imitates vertical and horizontal lines with a pencil.
- Makes a "snake" with clay.
- Screws lids on jars.

- Dresses himself, but often needs assistance.
- Has a great sense of order and neatness; does not like change.
- Is easily frustrated.
- Plays same thing at same time with other children, but there is little interaction or cooperation.
- Understands past *(last night)*, present *(now)*, and future *(tomorrow, someday)*.
- Understands *one, two,* and *many*.
- Counts two or more objects.
- Uses phrases or sentences containing four to six words.

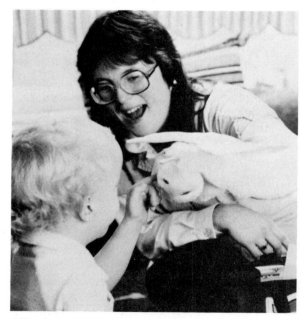

A friendly puppet can inspire toddlers to speak.

Household Playthings

Many commercially made toys make fine playthings, but there's no guarantee your toddler will like them. It can be frustrating to see your child ignore an expensive toy! You can avoid the expense and frustration by using items you already have at home. There are many things around your house that can become safe, fascinating toys for your toddler. And if she puts any of these aside, you can retrieve them for your own use. Here's a list of items with their uses:

- *Old-fashioned wooden clothespins and an empty coffee can or small-necked plastic bottle.* The child drops the pins into the bottle or attaches them along the rim of the can (file and tape any sharp edges).
- *Empty spools of thread.* The child stacks them, builds with them, strings them, and decorates them with paint or crayons.
- *Empty milk cartons, cans, and small boxes.* The child builds with them and puts things into them.
- *Plastic containers and lids.* The child stacks and nests them; she removes and replaces the lids.
- *Old coffee percolator.* The child takes it apart and puts it back together.
- *Old radios and gadgets (without small detachable parts).* The child watches parts move in relation to each other; she takes apart gadgets.
- *Stones and rocks (larger than 1" diameter).* The child examines and counts them, decorates them with paint or crayon, and makes designs with them.
- *Paste and scrap materials (small boxes, old jewelry, fabric scraps, colored paper, old greeting cards).* The child compares textures and colors, and pastes together materials to form two- and three-dimensional collages.
- *Lightweight hammer, softwood, and nails (to be supervised closely).* The child hammers nails and pulls them out with the claw.
- *Kitchen gadgets (sifters, hand beaters, pots and pans, measuring utensils, timers, plastic basters).* The child manipulates objects, plays house, and uses them as rhythm instruments.
- *Unbreakable dishes and cooking utensils.* The child manipulates the objects to prepare, serve, and eat imaginary meals.
- *Broom, dustpan, dustcloth, mop.* The child manipulates the objects to help with household tasks or to engage in pretend play.
- *Bathtub or large container, and water toys (cups, funnels, squeeze bottles, sprinkling can, spoons, straws, sponges).* The child transfers water from the objects to the tub, or from object to object; she watches objects float and sink; she retrieves floating objects.
- *Adult clothes.* The child names the clothing, matches it to body parts, dresses in loose-fitting garments, and engages in pretend play.
- *Cardboard tubes from toilet paper and paper towels.* The child looks through them, drops things through them, and makes sounds into them.
- *Old magazines.* The child names objects and talks about people, things, and activities in the pictures.
- *Large baskets and boxes.* The child crawls through a large box that has had its ends removed; she hides in a basket or box lying on its side; she uses containers as a house or cage during imaginative play.
- *Old furniture (sturdy tables, chairs, sofas, mattresses).* The child climbs over, under, around, and onto stable objects; she jumps onto and off of sofas, chairs, and mattresses; she creates playhouses and imaginary animals or vehicles to "ride on."

Educating on a Shoestring

If you have some spare moments in your busy day, you can put together simple and inexpensive toys for your child to use. Following are directions for making different playthings and ideas on how to introduce these homemade toys to your toddler. An appropriate age range is given for each plaything. When you put together a toy, keep in mind the safety hints suggested in the "Toys" section of *Health and Safety*.

Washcloth Puppet *(18-24 Months)*
To your child, bathtime probably means playtime. He enjoys splashing the water and playing with floating toys. But no matter how much he likes the bath, he may protest wildly when you get down to the business of washing his body. A washcloth puppet can help make bathtime more palatable.

To make a puppet, simply fold a washcloth in half. Sew the edges together along the open side and one end, leaving the other end open to slip your hand into. Sew on pieces of felt or large buttons (larger than 1" diameter) for eyes and a nose near the closed end of the mitt.

Give your puppet a name, such as Scrubs. Help your toddler become acquainted with Scrubs. Then use the puppet to wash your child's body, or let Scrubs rub your child's shampooed hair. Your child may also want to slip Scrubs on his own hand to wash himself.

Sorting Boxes *(18-24 Months)*
Homemade sorting boxes make terrific toys. Your child can not only use them for matching and sorting shapes, but also shake them to make a loud racket, take the lids off and put them back on, and build towers with them. If you begin with a pair of simple sorting boxes, you can eventually add more difficult ones to match his increasing sorting skills.

Use two containers that have plastic lids, such as potato-chip tubes, coffee cans, shortening containers, or margarine tubs. Make sure there are no sharp edges. Trace a cube-shaped building block on the plastic lid of one container, and cut out the square that you traced. Cut a hole in the lid of the other container that is large enough for a Ping-Pong ball to fit through. Then put the lids on the containers.

Show your child how to push the ball through the round hole. He will probably catch on to this task easily. It will be harder for him to fit the block through the square hole, since he will need to line up the corners.

Once your toddler becomes skilled with the two sorting boxes, add more difficult ones, introducing only one new sorting box at a time. You might construct boxes for sorting postcards, triangular blocks, or even cups from a tea set.

Bag Blocks *(18-24 Months)*
If you have lots of paper bags and old newspapers around your house, you can recycle them by making giant bag blocks. Large grocery bags make the best blocks, but you can also use other kinds of bags of various sizes. Besides bags and newspapers, you will need masking tape.

To make each block, crumple sheets of newspaper and stuff them into a bag until it is nearly full. Then fold over the open end and tape it shut. Make at least 10 bag blocks — the more the better.

Pile the giant blocks in a mound. Your child can jump on them, throw them into the air, hide under them, or toss them to you. He will especially enjoy playing with giant blocks when other children can share in the fun. Two or three toddlers can have a great time just rolling around on the blocks.

Paint Bags *(18-24 Months)*
Paint bags are an enjoyable alternative to
finger paint. They are easy to make with
common kitchen supplies, and you can
save them in the refrigerator to reuse
several times.

You will need some plastic bags (preferably
sandwich bags), ketchup, mustard,
puddings, and a roll of tape. To make the
paint bags, simply put a tablespoon of
ketchup, mustard, or pudding into each
bag and tape it shut. Lay each finished bag
flat on a table and tape all four corners to
the table.

Invite your child to slide his fingers across
the paint bags. As he experiments with
them, label the colors and talk about what
he is doing. Show him how to wipe his
hand across a bag to make the marks
disappear.

Make dots on a bag for your child to copy. If
he needs help copying the dots, hold his
pointed finger and make dots with him.
Also make lines and circles for him to
imitate.

A Senses Book *(18-24 Months)*
You can make a delightful senses book for
your child with colorful pictures that he can
look at, label, feel, and smell. You will need
old magazines or greeting cards, scissors,
nontoxic paste, construction paper, and a
stapler. You will also need items that he can
smell or touch when he looks at the
pictures. These might include perfume,
extract of mint, almond, or vanilla, pieces
of furry or satiny fabric, sandpaper, bark,
dried grass, flowers, and leaves. A short
trip outdoors will give you lots of other
ideas.

Cut out colored pictures from the
magazines or greeting cards that show
single objects or very simple scenes. Paste

Making noise — and letting off some steam.

each picture to a piece of construction
paper. Then select items that somehow
match the pictures. For example, you might
spray a flower picture with perfume or
paste a furry piece to a bear picture. Match
only one type of material to each picture.
Assemble the papers into a stack. Put on a
cover and staple the pages together to form
a book. Paste any leftover scraps of feely
materials onto the cover. Then look at the
book with your toddler!

Tot Towel *(18-24 Months)*
Whenever you help your child wash his
hands, let him dry them by himself. The
task will be easier for him if you hang a "tot
towel" from a doorknob or a low hook. The
towel will be easy for him to reach, and it
will hang securely when he wipes his
hands.

You will need a hand towel and a 12" piece
of rope or heavy cotton cord. To assemble
the tot towel, fold one short end of the
towel over the cord and sew the edge to the
towel. Then gather the sewn edge of the

towel and tie the ends of the cord together to form a handle:

Hang the towel from a doorknob or hook so that your child can reach it easily.

After you wash your child's hands, surprise him with the towel. Wipe your hands on it and ask him to do it, too. Offer help if he needs it and then tell him to try it by himself again.

Homemade Props for Playing House (24-30 Months)
A two-year-old is ready to enjoy pretend play, an activity at which children excel. House play is the most popular type of pretend play, since most children want to imitate the activities they see adults doing every day. After all, the desire to be like "big" people is very strong in children. You can invest quite a bit of money in toys for house play. Although this is money well spent, you can also make many of the same props.

Pretend Kitchen
- *Stove:* Stand a cardboard box bottom-end-up and draw burners with a marker pen.
- *Sink:* Use a plastic bowl with a lip on the rim. Turn another cardboard box bottom-end-up. Cut a hole in it that is slightly smaller than the rim on the bowl. Lower the bowl into the hole so that it forms the basin of the sink.
- *Refrigerator:* Use a rectangular cardboard box. Stand it on one of its smaller ends with the open end facing away from you. Cut a door in the side that faces you.

Stacking boxes can be a challenge.

- *Kitchen items:* Stock the kitchen with empty food containers such as cans, cereal boxes, egg cartons, and plastic containers.

Baby Doll Equipment
- *Bed:* Put an old diaper in an empty shoe box.
- *Bottle:* Use an empty glue bottle with a squeeze top.
- *Furniture:* Recycle your child's outgrown baby furniture (stroller, infant seat, baby bath) into doll furniture.

Shopping Equipment
- *Store displays:* Turn several cardboard boxes bottom-end-up. Stock these display tables with dress-up clothes, empty food containers, toys, and household odds and ends.
- *Play money:* Cut green paper into rectangles. Poker chips or checkers (larger than 1" diameter) can serve as coins. Place these in a shoe box to serve as a register. Put some empty paper bags near the register.

Wearing "Wings" (24-30 Months)
Props and costumes nearly always inspire pretend play. You can make a pair of wings that your child can use to become a soaring bird, a fluttery butterfly, a magical fairy, or

a daring superhero. You will need masking tape, scissors, and a roll of crepe paper.

Cut two 12" strips of masking tape. Then cut eight streamers of crepe paper that are each about 24" long. (They don't need to be equal in length.) Attach one end of each crepe-paper streamer to the sticky side of a tape strip — four to each strip. Leave some sticky space free along the top of the tape:

Tape the strips along your child's arms so that the crepe-paper streamers hang down when he holds out his arms. Then ask him to "fly" with his new wings.

Note: In a pretend activity like "flying," be sure to emphasize to your child that he can't really fly. Toddlers cannot always tell the difference between fantasy and reality.

Texture Cans (*24-30 Months*)
Instead of throwing away your empty food cans, make them into attractive building toys for your child. He can stack them to make towers, or nest them into each other. If you paste textured materials to them, he will compare the way they feel and enjoy the pretty colors and patterns.

Choose cans of various sizes. Find scraps of fabric, wrapping paper, lace, and ribbons. Wrap the scraps around the cans and paste them in place. File down and tape any sharp edges.

Show your child three cans and help him stack them in a tower, from big to little. Talk about the colors and textures on the cans, and label their sizes as he builds the tower. When he can build a big-to-little tower by himself, show him how to nest the cans. Help him place the middle-sized can in the big can and then put the little can in the middle-sized one.

Add more cans to his collection if he enjoys building with them.

Music Makers (*24-30 Months*)
With a homemade instrument, your toddler can accompany family songfests. He might also like to make up his own music. You can make the following simple instruments using household materials.

- *Banjo:* Slip several rubberbands around an empty facial-tissue box. Your child can strum with his fingers or a spoon.
- *Clickers:* Show your child how to make clicking sounds with a pair of tongs or a nutcracker.
- *Drum:* Any unbreakable object can be a drum — a plastic bowl, an empty coffee can, a shoe box. But a heavy aluminum pie plate makes a terrific drum because of its clear, loud sound.
- *Horn:* An empty toilet-paper or paper-towel roll makes a good horn. Show your child how to hum into the roll to make a musical sound.
- *Cymbals:* Glue empty spools to the inside of jar lids to make handles for a pair of cymbals. They make a delightful clang.
- *Maracas:* Put buttons or beans into a plastic container and make sure that the lid is taped and sealed tight!

Color Creatures (*24-30 Months*)
For this matching game you need three boxes with lids (shoe boxes are excellent). Make the lid on each box a different color — for example, red, blue, and yellow. You can either paint the lids or paste a piece of colored construction paper to each one. Draw eyes and noses on the lids to turn the boxes into "Color Creatures":

Then find a number of household articles that are red, blue, and yellow, such as red, blue, and yellow crayons, a red apple, a banana, a blue ribbon, a red comb, a yellow cup, and a blue bell.

Place the Color Creatures side by side on a table facing your child. Put all the objects within easy reach. Hold up an object, label the color, and "feed" the object to the matching creature by lifting the lid and putting the object into the box. Match several objects and then ask your child to try it.

Boats (30-36 Months)
Boats are easy to make, and your toddler will have a lot of fun playing with them. A boat in the bathtub can be a special treat (see Activity 15 in *Bathtime Business*). They are also fun to float in a swimming pool, a rain puddle, or even a dishpan of water. Choose from the following kinds.

Sailboats
Sailboats can be made out of a cork, walnut shell, jar lid, or bar of floating soap. To make a sail you'll need glue, scissors, playdough (or chewing gum), a toothpick (look for ones with rounded tops), and construction paper.

Cut a triangle out of construction paper and glue it onto the toothpick. If you are using a jar lid or walnut shell, place a ball of playdough in the center and stick the toothpick sail into the playdough. The toothpick sail can be stuck directly into the cork or soap. If you are using a cork, make a slit in the bottom and insert a penny to stabilize it.

Log Raft
To make a raft, you'll need seven twigs of equal thickness that are about 6" long. You'll also need some white glue, playdough, wax paper, and a sheet of plain white paper.

Place six of the twigs on a sheet of wax paper. Glue them together and let the glue dry overnight. Place a clump of playdough in the center of the raft. Cut a sail from the white paper and make a hole in each end of the paper. Attach it to the remaining twig:

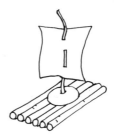

Insert the twig into the playdough and secure it. Your child may enjoy coloring the sail before you attach it to the twig.

Carpenter Boards (30-36 Months)
Few children would turn down an opportunity to use "grown-up" tools, and they have a special appeal if other family members often work with tools. Hammering nails and screwing screws is a good activity for developing eye-hand coordination.

Hammer Board
You'll need a piece of softwood (pine) and a lightweight hammer. Hammer six flathead nails into the wood, about a quarter of the way in:

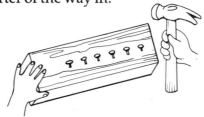

Ask your child to sit on the floor. Place the hammer board and hammer in front of him and ask him what they are. Show your child how to hold the hammer in his dominant hand and the end of the board in his other hand. Ask him to choose one nail to hammer down. Encourage him to

Pointing to pictures.

hammer it all the way before starting on another one.

Screw Board
Screw six large screws into a piece of softwood. Screw them all the way down so holes are made and then screw them out about halfway.

Show your child the screwdriver and the board. Show him how to put the screwdriver into the groove of the screw and how to turn the handle. Help him position the screwdriver in his dominant hand and use his other hand to help secure his grasp. You may need to place your hands over his and help him turn the handle a few times until he gets the idea.

Dominoes (*30-36 Months*)
By playing dominoes your child can learn to identify and match different objects, designs, colors, shapes, and figures. To make dominoes, cut cardboard into twenty 2" x 4" rectangles. Draw a line down the middle of each piece:

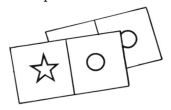

Next, decide what subject area you want to work on with your child: shapes? colors? animals? household objects? If, for example, you choose colors, select five (red, yellow, blue, green, black) to work on. Draw or cut out eight 2" x 2" pictures of each of the five colors you choose.

Draw or paste the pictures onto the cards so there are two pictures on each card. A few cards can have identical pictures on them, but most should have a different picture on each side. Colors and shapes can be drawn on the cards fairly easily. If you want to make animal dominoes or common-object dominoes, you can buy booklets of stamps with these pictures on them. They are inexpensive and are sold in card shops and bookstores.

See Activity 15 in *Teaching — Family Style* for directions for playing a game of dominoes.

Lacing Boards (*30-36 Months*)
If your child watches you intently when you lace his shoes, he'll love to try a lacing board. It is a great activity for developing eye-hand coordination. To make lacing boards, you need cardboard, tape, shoelaces, and a hole punch.

Cut some simple figures out of the cardboard, such as a hat, a house, an ice-cream cone, or an animal. Punch holes along the edge of each picture:

Use shoelaces to lace around each picture.

Show one of the cards to your child and talk about what the figure is. Then show him how to lace around the card, using a loop stitch (always putting the lace through the top of the hole). Leave the last three holes unsewn and let your toddler give it a try. Show him how to hold the lace in his dominant hand, near the top between his thumb and forefinger. Let him try lacing on his own. If he needs some help, guide his hand or tell him which hole is next and remind him to put the lace through the top.

A simple baster teaches both fine-motor and cognitive skills.

Recommended Readings

Ames, L. B., and Ilg, F. L. *Your two year old: Terrible or tender*. New York: Delacorte Press, 1976.

Biller, H., and Meredith, D. *Father power*. New York: Doubleday & Co., 1975.

Braga, J., and Braga, L. *Children and adults: Activities for growing together*. Englewood Cliffs, New Jersey: Prentice-Hall, 1976.

Brazelton, T. *Toddlers and parents: A declaration of independence*. New York: Delacorte Press, 1974.

Caplan, F., and Caplan, T. *The second twelve months of life: A kaleidoscope of growth*. New York: Grosset & Dunlap, 1977.

Dinkmeyer, D., and McKay, G. *The parent's handbook: Systematic training for effective parenting*. Circle Pines, Minnesota: American Guidance Service, 1982.

Dodson, F. *How to father*. New York: New American Library, 1975.

Dodson, F. *How to parent*. New York: New American Library, 1973.

Dreikurs, F., and Soltz, V. *Children: The challenge*. New York: Meredith Press, 1964.

Fraiberg S. *The magic years: Understanding and handling the problems of early childhood*. New York: Charles Scribner's Sons, 1959.

Gordon, T. *Parent effectiveness training: The tested new way to raise responsible children*. New York: Peter H. Wyden, 1970.

Kelly, M., and Parsons, E. *The mother's almanac*. Garden City, New York: Doubleday & Co., 1975.

Lansky, V. *The taming of the C.A.N.D.Y. monster*. Wayzata, Minnesota: Meadowbrook Press, 1978.

Loebl, S., and Ria, S. *Parents magazine's mother's encyclopedia and everyday guide to family health*. New York: Dell Publishing Co., 1981.

Marzollo, J. *Supertot: Creative learning activities for children from one to three and sympathetic advice for their parents*. New York: Harper & Row, 1977.

McDiarmid, N. J.; Peterson, M. A.; and Sutherland, J. R. *Loving and learning: Interacting with your child from birth to three*. New York: Harcourt Brace Jovanovich, 1975.

Newson, J., and Newson, E. *Toys and playthings*. New York: Pantheon, 1979.

Olness, K., M.D. *Raising happy healthy children*. Wayzata, Minnesota: Meadowbrook Press, 1977.

Rubin, R. R.; Fisher, J. J. III; and Doering, S. G. *Your toddler: Ages one and two*. New York: Macmillan Publishing Co., 1980.

Sullivan, S. A. *The father's almanac*. Garden City, New York: Doubleday & Co., 1980.

Watrin, R., and Furfey, P. H. *Learning activities for the young preschool child*. New York: D. Van Nostrand Co., 1978.

White, B. L. *A parent's guide to the first three years*. Englewood Cliffs, New Jersey: Prentice-Hall, 1980.

Just for the Two of You

1. Saying Sounds
2. Putting "Baby" to Bed
3. Lullaby and Goodnight
4. Brushing Teeth
5. Buttoning and Zipping
6. Story Time
7. Getting Ready for Bed
8. Getting Dressed
9. Naming Feelings
10. Expressing Feelings
11. Naming Sounds
12. Scooping Balls
13. What's Missing?
14. Identifying Objects by Touch
15. Patterning
16. Getting Ready to Use the Toilet
17. Using the Toilet

1. SAYING SOUNDS

Age Range
18-24 months

Materials
• Storybooks with colorful pictures
• Magazines

The books you look at with your child should be very simple picture books. A book showing a single object on each page is still best for this age group. If your toddler enjoys naming the objects as you look at the pictures together, he* would probably enjoy making some sounds, too.

Choose a book with pictures of "noisy objects" such as animals, vehicles, a telephone, a clock, a bell, a drum, and a horn. You can purchase the book, borrow one from the library, or cut out magazine pictures and make the book yourself.

As you look through the book with your toddler, ask him to label each picture. Then tell him what sound the object makes: **"This big drum says, 'Boom, boom, boom.'"** Ask him to say the sound after you: **"Can you say the sound of the drum? Say, 'Boom, boom, boom.' Yes, you sound like the big drum."**

Repeat the sounds whenever you sit down with your toddler and a storybook. When he seems to know the sounds, ask him to say them without any hints from you: **"Here's the drum. What does the drum say? That's right! 'Boom, boom.'"**

Don't overlook other informal opportunities to foster your toddler's cognitive and verbal development. While looking at your favorite magazine, show the pictures to him and encourage him to point to items that make sounds.

Saying what you say.

2. PUTTING "BABY" TO BED

Age Range
18-24 months

Materials
• Baby doll

Both boys and girls will enjoy giving tender loving care to a baby doll. A child can pretend to be mom or dad and use the baby to act out familiar family events. And when your toddler needs comfort, she* can give her doll extra hugs and snuggles. At bedtime, encourage her to prepare her own baby for bed. She will enjoy imitating you as caregiver, and taking care of baby may help her face bedtime more cheerfully.

Suggest that your toddler care for her baby as you help her get washed up and ready for bed: **"It's time for you and baby to go to bed now. Help baby get ready."** If your child needs a bath, let her wash the doll while she's in the tub. She might also feed baby a bedtime snack, brush the baby's teeth, help you dress the baby, and comb its hair. **"Comb baby's hair now. It looks**

---

*In odd-numbered activities, the toddler is referred to as a boy. In even-numbered activities, the toddler is referred to as a girl.

---

*In even-numbered activities, the toddler is referred to as a girl. In odd-numbered activities, the toddler is referred to as a boy.

so pretty. **Now you let me comb your hair. You and baby look nice!"**

Encourage your child to tuck the doll into bed and kiss it goodnight. She may have a doll bed for the baby to sleep in, or she may want to sleep with the doll in her own bed.

Taking care of a doll or stuffed animal encourages self-help skills.

3. LULLABY AND GOODNIGHT

Age Range
18-24 months

Materials
• None

After you finish looking through the last bedtime storybook with your child, end the day with a lullaby. A soothing, singsong voice will help put him in a sleepy mood. And he will enjoy a last, lingering hug from you while you recite the rhyme.

You may have a favorite lullaby, or you might try the following one. Hold your toddler in your arms while you say the following poem, and do the actions as they are described in the verse, changing the words if you have a little girl:

Rock-a, rock-a
Sleepy boy.
Kiss his pretty head.

Sweetly, sweetly
Give a hug.
Tuck him into bed.

Don't be self-conscious about your voice — your toddler thinks that everything you do is marvelous.

4. BRUSHING TEETH

Age Range
18-24 months

Materials
• Your toothbrush and toddler's toothbrush
• Toothpaste*

When it's time for your child to wash up after meals, encourage her to do as much for herself as possible. Brushing teeth is a task that requires a lot of coordination, and your child is probably not ready to do this job alone. But you can show her how to help as you brush her teeth for her.

Some young children resist having their teeth brushed; others are fascinated with the process. If your child does dislike the task, invite her to help you prepare her toothbrush. This might ease her resistance a bit. First, hold the toothbrush and ask her to help you squeeze the paste onto it. Be prepared! Once she gets the hang of it, let her hold the brush while you squeeze the tube with her.

With your own toothbrush, show your toddler how you move the brush up and

*Do not use fluoridated toothpaste if your child swallows most of the toothpaste. The amount of fluoride received can be excessive, causing tooth mottling later on. (Children should be receiving the correct fluoride dose in fluoridated water or fluoride supplements.)

down on your teeth. Don't expect her to brush her teeth skillfully — just to move the brush around a little in her mouth. **"You made your front teeth look so clean. Let me brush the back ones for you."** When you're finished, let your child hold her brush under the running water to rinse it off. ✸

5. BUTTONING AND ZIPPING

Age Range
18-24 months

Materials
- Jacket with zipper
- Sweater with buttons
- Ring (optional)

Your child's desire to touch and investigate everything he sees is part of his learning experience. Your own clothing has lots of intriguing items that he would love to manipulate — zippers, buttons, hooks, snaps, jewelry. Sometime when you have on a jacket with a zipper or a sweater with large buttons, have him sit on your lap and work the fasteners.

If you are wearing something with buttons, button one of them halfway. Then tell your toddler to finish it: **"Look at this button, (child's name). Would you finish buttoning it? Push it through the hole."** Buttons on sweaters are easier than those on shirts, blouses, or coats because the knit fabric stretches easily when your child pushes the button through. At first he will need help, but after he practices a few times he might be able to push the button completely through the hole by himself.

Put on a jacket with a large zipper and zip it up an inch or two. Then hold the zipper taut and invite your child to zip it open and shut. Emphasize the words *open, closed, up,* and *down* as he pulls the tab: **"Pull the tab**

up. **That's it. Now my zipper is** *closed.* **Can you open the zipper? That's right. Pull it** *down.***"**

If you wear a ring, put it on your little finger. Then let your child pull it off and put it back on. **"*Off* comes the ring. Now put it *on* again. Can you put the ring *on* your finger? *Off* again. *On* again."** Supervise closely because rings may end up in the child's mouth. ✸

6. STORY TIME

Age Range
24-30 months

Materials
• Favorite storybooks

Sometimes story time is a quiet time when your child can relax and listen. But at other times she will participate actively — answering your questions, naming pictured items, and pointing to things that you name. The following are suggestions you can use to encourage your toddler's participation during story sessions.

Taking part in storytelling.

Read a simple story that your child especially enjoys and is familiar with. After each page ask her to point to different characters: **"Show me Little Red Riding Hood."** Then name objects in the pictures and ask her to point them out: **"Where is Red Riding Hood's basket?"**

After a story, point to different characters in the pictures and ask your child to identify them: **"Who's that? Yes, it's the wolf!"**

After a page that has lots of action, ask questions about what is happening. Use the pictures to help clarify your questions. For example, you might show your child a picture of the wolf in grandma's bed and ask, **"Who's in grandma's bed? That's not grandma! Yes, it's the wolf. Does Red Riding Hood know that the wolf is in grandma's bed?"** Your child will not be able to answer all of your questions. When she doesn't, say the answer yourself. Eventually, after she hears your questions many times, she will begin to answer more of them.

When your child is very familiar with a story, pause before turning a page and ask what will happen next. For example: **"Suddenly the wolf jumped out of bed — and what did he do? Did he take a bath? No, what did he do?"**

At other times look at picture books your child is not familiar with. Ask her to identify objects that you describe in the pictures: **"Show me the dog in the fire engine."**

7. GETTING READY FOR BED

Age Range
24-30 months

Materials
• Picture book, puzzle, or photo album

Most toddlers do not face bedtime willingly. There are just too many interesting things to do. Besides, lying in bed can be a lonely and frightening experience for a young child. You can help your child face bedtime by establishing a bedtime routine. If he knows what to expect at bedtime, he may accept it more readily.

Decide on a time, and make that your child's regular bedtime. About one-half hour before, tell him that in a few minutes it will be time to get ready for bed. When that time comes, say, **"The *clock* says it's time for bed."**

Tell your toddler that after he gets washed up and dressed in his pajamas you will do something special together. Plan a quiet activity — reading a book, working a puzzle, or looking at the family picture album. You both might enjoy a goodnight lullaby or a short talk. Talk about the things your child did during the day and what might happen tomorrow.

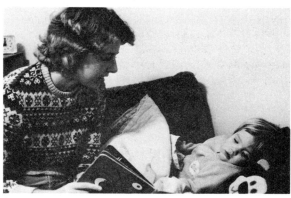
A quiet story before turning out the light.

Tuck your toddler into bed with lots of hugs and kisses and I-love-yous.

If your child cries after you leave his room, he may be afraid of the dark or of monsters. Or he may just miss your company. Leave a night light or a closet light on, or suggest that he sleep with a favorite toy animal or doll. A family dog or cat might also stay in the room and keep him company. Check on your child every few minutes until he is asleep so that he feels you are close by.

Many young children awake during the night. There are several common reasons for night waking: noises in the house from a television, stereo set, furnace, or other household sources; discomfort from thirst, hunger, heat, or cold; nightmares or fears of the dark. If your child does wake up, comfort him back to sleep in his own bed. If you let him stay up or get into bed with you, you will only encourage a regular habit of this. If sleep problems continue for more than a week or two, it's a good idea to consult your pediatrician for extra suggestions. 🏃

8. GETTING DRESSED

Age Range
24-30 months

Materials
• Articles of clothing

Before your toddler can dress herself, she must have both the motor ability to do the task and the desire to take care of herself. Sometimes it's very comforting to have mom or dad do the job, even if she *can* do it alone. Of course many dressing tasks are too difficult for a child of this age to do, but you should encourage her to try the easiest dressing chores by herself.

Choose an article of clothing that is easy to put on, and teach your toddler how to do it step-by-step. You might have her try pajama bottoms or pants with an elasticized waist, a loose-fitting robe, an undershirt, or a v-neck pullover.

At dressing time, describe the steps of putting on the piece of clothing you've chosen. For example, if you are dressing her in an undershirt you might say, **"First we put your arm in this sleeve; this arm goes in the other sleeve. We put the shirt** over your head. **Here comes your head through the hole. Now I'll pull the shirt down over your tummy.''**

When you want her to try it alone, dress her yourself until the last step. Then ask her to do that part: **''Now pull the shirt over your tummy all by yourself. You did it. What a big girl!''** When she has mastered the last step, have her try the next-to-last step, too. It will probably take several months before she can do the entire job by herself.

Learning how to pull down a sweater.

9. NAMING FEELINGS

Age Range
24-30 months

Materials
- Pictures of people or animals expressing various emotions

Learning how to handle personal feelings is a lifetime process. A first step in dealing with feelings is knowing how to name them. Now that your toddler can use words, teach him the names for some basic emotions, such as happy, sad, and angry.

When your child shows emotion, take a moment to name his feelings for him: **''You look happy. You like splashing in the tub!''** Also name your own feelings: **''I lost my watch! I feel sad.''**

At story time, find pictures of characters expressing clear emotions and ask your toddler how they might feel: **''Look at the elephant's tears. How do you think he feels right now?''**

10. EXPRESSING FEELINGS

Age Range
24-30 months

Materials
- None

Once your young child can recognize and name some of her feelings, you can begin to help her express these feelings in appropriate ways. Dealing with emotions is a tough job, and so it will take time and patience on your part. The following are some suggestions that might help you. Remember that everyone is different; eventually you will learn which of these suggestions work best with your child.

When your child expresses an emotion, give it a name: **"You look angry. Your face has a big frown on it."** Then help her express her feelings with words. In any emotional situation, talk about her feelings and teach her phrases she can use to express herself: **"You might feel better if you say, 'I'm angry (mad).'"**

Sometimes words aren't enough. If your child needs to express her feelings physically, find an "angry corner" that she can use. An "angry corner" is an empty corner of a room where she can swing her arms, kick, cry, or shout. Let her know that this behavior is appropriate only in her "angry corner." Whenever your child is in her corner, everyone else should leave her alone.

After your toddler expresses her feelings, help her find ways to cope with the situation that caused the feelings. For example, if she is angry because you took a dangerous object away from her, help her find something safe to play with. If she is frustrated because she can't get her shoes on by herself, show her how to do the task step-by-step.

If your child makes a scene in a public place, you may feel helpless, angry, and embarrassed. First of all, keep in mind that it happens to nearly every parent at some time. The best way to deal with your child is to remove her from the area (store, playground, babysitter's home, or wherever). While you are leading or carrying her away, talk about her feelings: **"I know you want to buy a toy, but not today. You really sound angry."** You are letting your child know that her feelings are okay, but that her inappropriate behavior won't change the situation. 🏃

An angry toddler may need to be held and comforted.

11. NAMING SOUNDS

Age Range
30-36 months

Materials
- Noisemakers: bell, horn, drum, whistle, hair dryer
- Tape recorder (optional)

It is important for your toddler to have all of his senses stimulated — seeing, feeling, hearing, smelling, and tasting. You may feel he doesn't need much help when it comes to touching and tasting things. It's likely he has touched more things than you can count and has tasted many things you wish he hadn't! But activities in these areas are still beneficial and fun, so don't overlook opportunities. Activities in listening are also beneficial. This may seem especially true when it is time to come inside for the night or time to put toys away. For this listening activity, all you need are some noisemakers that your child is familiar with.

Sit at a table with your child. Place all the objects in front of him and let him make noise with each one. Then play each one for him, naming the object as you play it. **"Now let's play a game with these things. I will play one of them while you listen very carefully. Then you tell me what made the noise."**

Pick up one object and play it, holding it under the table so your child can't see it. (You may find yourself doing a disappearing act when it is time to blow the whistle or toot the horn.) If he isn't quite sure what made the noise, play it again. If he still isn't sure, show him the object and play it again: **"The drum made the sound."** Continue this procedure, using all the objects you have collected.

If you have a tape recorder, you can play another listening game with your toddler.

Name that sound!

Tape familiar household sounds such as water running, the phone ringing, a dog barking, a door closing, the electric mixer running, a baby crying, and the radio playing. Play the first sound for your child and then turn the recorder off. Ask him to identify the sound. If he isn't sure what it is, rewind the tape and play the sound again. Repeat this procedure for the other sounds.

12. SCOOPING BALLS

Age Range
30-36 months

Materials
- 2 plastic milk cartons or bleach containers
- Small rubber ball or whiffle ball

This game takes two people, two scoops, and one ball. You and your toddler fit the bill for two people. Two scoops can be made by cutting off the bottom of plastic milk cartons or bleach containers (tape any sharp edges). The ball can be purchased at a variety store. This game will help your child improve her coordination and will also give her an opportunity to be a partner in play.

Sit about 6' away from your toddler. Show her how to place the scoop flat on the floor so the opening is facing you. Position your scoop the same way so the opening is facing her. Explain, **"We are going to play a game of catch. But instead of catching the ball with our hands, we're going to use these scoops. Hold your scoop steady so that I can roll the ball into it."** After you have rolled the ball, ask her to take the ball out of her scoop and roll it into your scoop. Move your scoop if it looks as if the ball isn't going to make it in. Continue playing the game of catch as long as your child is interested.

13. WHAT'S MISSING?

Age Range
30-36 months

Materials
- Pictures of people
- Scissors
- Full-length mirror and towel (optional)

Over the past two and one-half years your child has been learning the names of lots of things. Among the words he's learned are the names of body parts. You've probably spent a good deal of time pointing at your child, yourself, and pictures in books, asking "What's this?" Once he is naming body parts as fast as you can point, the time is ripe to introduce a new activity — naming a body part that is missing from a figure. He will be developing his language skills as well as learning about parts and wholes.

Cut out a full-length picture of a person from a magazine and then cut the figure apart, separating the body parts (arms, legs, head, trunk, feet, hands). On a table in front of your child, arrange the body parts and say, **"Let's play a game with this picture of a person. Before we play, I'm going to point to different body parts on the figure and I'd like you to tell me their names."** Point to each body part for him to name. **"Now cover your eyes with your hands and don't peek. I'm going to take one body part off the figure. When I tell you it's okay to look, you tell me which body part is missing from the figure."** Follow this procedure until you have removed each body part at least once and he has named the missing part.

Naming — and finding — the missing body part.

Give your toddler a chance to remove a body part for you to identify. You can also give him all the body-part pieces and let him put them together to form the figure of the person. He may need some help with the activity, though. Encourage him to find the head and place it on the table first. Point to your body as he puts each of the other parts on — trunk, arms, hands, legs, feet. You can also help by asking your child questions such as

- "What is under my head?"
- "What is at the end of my arms?"
- "Are my legs to the side or under my body?"

As a variation, stand in front of a mirror with your toddler and use a towel to cover up a part of his body. Then ask what's missing. If he enjoys the game, continue with other body parts. 🧒

14. IDENTIFYING OBJECTS BY TOUCH

Age Range
30-36 months

Materials
- Paper bag
- Objects easily identified by touch: spoon, cup, book, ball, pencil, toy car, and fork

During the course of a day your child identifies many things by seeing them. Other times, several of her senses may work together to help her know what's going on around her. She may hear a bird sing and then see it perched in a tree, or smell cookies baking and then rush into the kitchen to watch you remove them from the oven. Since your toddler often uses several senses at a time to identify things, it can be fun and challenging to play games that require her to rely on only one of her senses. This game gives her an opportunity to rely on her sense of touch. It takes very little time to prepare for the activity, so it is a great game to play when you need something quick to do with your child.

Sit at a table with your toddler and place the objects in a row. Point to each one and ask her to name it. After she has identified the object, ask her to pick it up and encourage her to feel all parts of it. Describe how it feels: **"It's easy to tell this is a book because it has lots of pages. The fork is long and has four sharp points on one end."**

After your child has examined each object, place them on the floor. Hold the paper bag under the table and place one item inside. Be sure she doesn't see which thing you've chosen. **"I've put one of the objects in this bag. I'd like you to tell me what's inside, but you can't look in the bag. Put your hands inside and tell me what it is by feeling it."** Open the bag just enough for your child to slip her hands inside. You may want to ask her to close her eyes while the bag is open to make sure she doesn't see the object.

Ask your toddler to tell you what she feels. If she isn't sure, ask her to tell you how it feels: **"Is it round and smooth? Is it long with one point on the end?"** When she identifies it, give her three cheers for a job well done. She may enjoy the fuss you made over her accomplishment so much that she will be eager to continue. You can reward her another way by putting a "prize" in the bag that she can keep and play with. Toddlers are old enough to appreciate such thoughtfulness. Play the game as long as she is interested. 🧒

15. PATTERNING

Age Range
30-36 months

Materials
- 4 each of spoons, forks, pencils, and blocks
- Bowl or box

Patterning involves two actions: looking at the way a group of objects is arranged and making the same arrangement with a similar group of objects. It's a good way for your toddler to sharpen his matching skills. It is also an opportunity to use the words *first* and *last* and to work from left to right, which is a prereading skill.

Put the objects in a bowl or box and sit next to your child on the floor. Explain, **"In this bowl I have some things for us to play with."** Hand him two objects: **"What did I give you? That's right! You have a spoon and a pencil. I am going to get a spoon and a pencil also. Watch what I do with my spoon and pencil."** Lay the spoon down and place the pencil to the right of the spoon. Point to each one and name it, going from left to right: **"Spoon . . . pencil."**

Try patterning with paper cut-outs.

Continue, **"Put your spoon and pencil down just like mine."** Point to the space below your spoon: **"Put your spoon right here."** When your child has put the spoon down, ask him, **"Where does your pencil go?"** If he isn't sure, point to your pattern: **"Spoon . . . pencil. Now, what goes here? That's right, the pencil."** Pick up all the objects and repeat the pattern. Then ask him to do the same thing below yours. If he has difficulty, point again to your pattern: **"Here's my spoon. It goes first. Put down your spoon first."**

When your toddler can make that pattern, try a new one using other objects. Make the pattern first and ask him to make his below yours. When he can readily copy patterns of two objects, try a pattern with three objects. Lay the objects down and name each one, moving from left to right. As he makes his pattern, compare it to yours: **"I put down a fork first; you put down a fork first. I put down a button; you put down a button."** 👫

16. GETTING READY TO USE THE TOILET

Age Range
30-36 months

Materials
- Books with pictures of toileting activities
- Potty chair or seat
- Doll

Using the toilet is a very complicated skill. Your child must be physically able to control her bladder and sphincter muscles. She must have the motor skill necessary to undress and dress herself. She must be able to understand your directions and to tell you when she needs to go or when she needs help. And she must have the maturity to want to be like a big person — to keep her pants dry, to wear underpants, and to take care of herself.

Right now you can watch for clues that your toddler is ready to take on this responsibility. Some signs of readiness include staying dry for long periods of time, concentrating while she wets or soils her diaper, showing interest when others use the toilet, and attempting to undress and dress herself.

When you think your toddler is ready, take your time and teach her toileting skills with patience. (Keep in mind that it usually takes several months for a child to learn how to use the toilet.) Try not to become anxious or frustrated — it will only turn toileting into a battle of wills. The following suggestions are some pretoileting activities that you can use with your child.

- Talk to your toddler matter-of-factly about her eliminations: **"Your diapers are wet. You urinated in them. I'll change you so you will have dry pants."**

- Encourage your child to use names for her eliminations: **"You have B.M. in your diaper. Say 'B.M.'"** If she knows the labels, she will be able to tell you when her diapers are soiled.

- Check your child's diaper often and try to change her soon after she eliminates. If she is accustomed to a dry diaper, she will be more conscious of soiling it.

- Find books that feature illustrations or photographs of toileting activities. Here's a chance for your toddler to observe others and name pictured items.

- Let your child watch others use the toilet (especially people of the same sex), so she can see how it's done.

- Introduce her to a potty seat. Either use an insert for the adult toilet seat or a child-size potty chair. (It's important that her feet reach the floor or a stepstool so that she's in the proper position to move her bowels effectively.) Use a doll to act out the use of the potty. (A doll that wets gives the most graphic picture.) Invite your child to help the doll use the

Reading a picture book about using the toilet.

potty. If she shows an interest, help her remove her own pants and sit on the potty, too. Don't expect her to eliminate in the potty — let her get used to it first.

- Help your child remove and put on her own outer pants when you change her diaper at dressing time. If possible, dress her in pants with elasticized waists that are easy to pull down.

- Be positive! And praise your child for any steps in the right direction.

17. USING THE TOILET

Age Range
30-36 months

Materials
- Potty chair or seat
- Training pants

Before you bring out the training pants, make sure that your child is physically and emotionally ready to use the toilet. The previous activity lists some kinds of behavior that indicate a child's readiness. The following suggestions will be helpful when you do begin toilet training with your child.

- Teach your toddler how to pull down his own pants and sit on the potty seat by himself. Using the toilet is a self-help skill. Expect your child to do as much as possible by himself. Of course, there will be times when he will need assistance in removing awkward clothing.

- When your child does eliminate in the toilet, tell him what he is doing and ask him to repeat the phrase after you. You might say, **"You're using the toilet. Say, 'I used the toilet.'"** In this way he will learn a term that he can eventually use to describe his use of the toilet.

- Use lots of praise. Praise your child for removing his own pants, for sitting on the potty, for staying on it, and for trying to eliminate. And when he does eliminate, he deserves lots and lots of praise.

- Once your child has had some successes, ask him occasionally if he needs to use the toilet. Be careful not to overdo it and become a nag — let your toddler learn to experience the "urge" to go. If he tells you that he needs to use the toilet, immediately tell him to go to the bathroom. Provide assistance only when needed and praise him lavishly for helping himself.

- Expect accidents and don't let them upset you. Simply have your child remove his soiled pants and help you with cleanup. But if you sense that his accidents aren't accidental, he might not be ready for the toilet. If he is very upset about using the toilet and has frequent accidents, postpone toilet training until he shows a willingness and interest in toileting.

- Once your child catches on and has regular success with the toilet, let him wear training pants instead of diapers, day and night. Emphasize that these are special pants for toilet-users: **"Look at these big-boy pants. You can wear them because you use the toilet. No more diapers for you."** Once he begins to wear training pants, let him wear them all the time. If you put him in diapers sometimes, he will be confused about his toilet responsibilities. Make sure that his mattress is protected and expect some wet nights.

- Your toddler might develop behavior problems at this time that seem totally unrelated to toileting — refusing to eat, tantruming, whining, or fighting with other children. Keep in mind that learning to use the toilet is a very difficult task. The strain on your child might be expressed in these other ways. Once he has the toilet mastered, his behavior will probably improve.

Just for the Fun of It

1. Imitating Actions
2. Inserting "Pegs" into Holes
3. Matching Objects
4. Building a Tower
5. Listening to a Story About Myself
6. Using a Pen
7. Lotto
8. Working with Clay
9. Hide-and-Seek
10. Using Props to Act Out a Story
11. Animal Sounds
12. Whispering
13. Stretching
14. Squeeze a Color/Squirt a Picture
15. Statues
16. Fun with a Flashlight
17. Paint-Stamping

1. IMITATING ACTIONS

Age Range
18-24 months

Materials
• 2 spoons or dowels

Your toddler learns a lot by imitating your actions. In order to imitate, he* must watch carefully, remember what he saw, and then use his body to perform the action. Toddlers love this sort of challenge! When you have a free moment, use two spoons or dowels to play an imitation game with your child.

First, play a "Do What I Do" game. Hand your child one of the spoons and ask him to do several things with you. For example, hit the spoon on the floor and ask him to do the same thing along with you. Say the following chant in a singsong voice to keep his interest:

> *Try to do what I do,*
> *I do, I do.*
> *Try to do what I do —*
> *Hit the floor.*

Toddlers enjoy imitating you as you crumple up aluminum foil.

You might do some other things together as you chant: gently tap your head (or other body parts) with the spoon, hold it behind your back, step on the spoon, or balance it on your head. Remember to give your child a chance to do some actions for *you* to copy.

Once your toddler can imitate your actions easily, challenge him to remember and repeat your movements. Hold both of the spoons and tap them together while you repeat the chant:

> *Try to do what I do,*
> *I do, I do.*
> *Try to do what I do —*
> *Tap the spoons.*

Then hand the spoons to him and ask him to do it. If he doesn't repeat your action, describe what you did: **"Tap the spoons together as I did. Tappity-tap."**

Do other actions for your toddler to remember and repeat: hold the spoons over your head, place them next to each other on the floor, or hold them up and drop them.

2. INSERTING "PEGS" INTO HOLES

Age Range
18-24 months

Materials
• Several empty spools of thread
• Several drinking straws

It takes lots of concentration and good eye-hand coordination for your child to fit a peg into a hole. When she* is a few months older, a pegboard will make a good

---

*In odd-numbered activities, the toddler is referred to as a boy. In even-numbered activities, the toddler is referred to as a girl.

*In even-numbered activities, the toddler is referred to as a girl. In odd-numbered activities, the toddler is referred to as a boy.

toy. Right now, you can show her how to fit larger "pegs" into holes — a simpler task.

Stand the spools in front of your child. Then insert a straw into the hole of one spool, saying, **"Look at this. I put the straw into the hole. You can do it, too!"** Point to another spool and say, **"Put a straw into this hole."** Hold the spool steady while she pushes the straw in. Take turns pushing straws into the rest of the spools.

Another simple pegboard: a shoe box and empty spools.

Once your toddler can do this task fairly well, make the game a little bit harder. Stand one spool on end and push a straw into the hole. Then push another spool onto the same straw. Ask her to finish stacking spools onto the straw: **"Look, we made a tower of spools!"** When the tower is finished, tell her to knock it over and start another one. 🏃

3. MATCHING OBJECTS

Age Range
18-24 months

Materials
- 2 identical objects and 1 similar object: 2 pencils and a pen, 2 toy cars and a truck, 2 envelopes and a sheet of paper
- 2 paper bags

Match-up activities call for important cognitive skills. Your toddler must look at objects carefully and compare them. To do this he must understand the concepts *same* and *different*, although he doesn't necessarily have to understand the two words. Even if he finds match-up games a great challenge, he will probably be interested for only a short time. So keep this type of activity short — about five minutes.

Put the sets of objects into a paper bag and give an empty bag to your child. Sit on the floor facing each other. Take two similar objects out of your bag (such as a pencil and a pen) and place them on the floor. Help him name the items. Then take the matching object out of the bag. Name the new object and ask your toddler to show you the mate: **"Look, here's a pencil. Do you see another pencil? Where is it? Yes, these pencils are the *same*."**

If your child does not respond, he may not understand what you want him to do. Try using visual cues to help him pick the matching object: **"Here's a pencil. Where's the other pencil? Here it is!** (Place pencils next to each other) **They're the same. A pencil . . . a pencil. Show me the pencils."**

After you and your child match the identical objects, let him put all three things into his bag. Continue the activity with the remaining sets of objects as long as he is interested. When you are finished, compare your two bags: **"Look, my bag is empty! You have lots of things in your bag."**

Keep this activity in mind for other times — when you're sorting laundry, drying dishes or silverware, or using tools. Take advantage of ordinary moments and turn them into something special for your toddler! ✸

Telling the difference between a sandal and a slipper.

4. BUILDING A TOWER

Age Range
18-24 months

Materials
- Building blocks
- Empty box or bag
- Heavy masking tape

Building a tower with blocks takes concentration and the ability to coordinate eye and hand movements. Because your toddler's attention span is still fairly short, this demanding task may interest her for only a short time. But if you add something exciting, she may stay interested longer than you.

To set up the activity, tape one side of the box or bag (open side up) to the edge of a table. Then build a tower with three blocks. Invite your child to sit at the table where she is close enough to reach the blocks and the hanging box. Point to the tower and say, **"Look at the tower I made. It's so tall. Uh-oh, I think it's going to fall!"** Knock over the tower and scoop the blocks into the box.

Ask your toddler to help you make another tower. Put one block on the table. Then hand her another block and show her where to put it. **"Good job! The tower is getting taller!"** Give her the third block and point to where it should go. When the tower is finished, congratulate her and ask her to knock it over. Then help her push the blocks off the table into the box.

Build several more towers, encouraging your child to do more and more of the task by herself. When she can do it alone, have her add a fourth block to the tower so that she can make a bigger crash. ✸

5. LISTENING TO A STORY ABOUT MYSELF

Age Range
18-24 months

Materials
- Doll

Bedtime can be a wonderful time to tell a story. This time, instead of using a storybook, use a doll to help you tell a story about your toddler.

First, introduce the doll to your child: **"This is a boy named (your child's name). I have a story to tell you about this little person."** Go on to make up a story about the things your child did during the day: **"When (Jesse) woke up this morning,** there was snow on the ground. After breakfast he played outside. He ran in the snow and rolled down the hill and threw snow up in the air. . . ."

After you finish, ask your toddler to repeat the events of the story: **"What did Jesse do today?"** If he needs a reminder, ask simple questions and give hints. End the story with bedtime: **"And finally Jesse got into his bed and went to sleep. Goodnight!"**

straight, curved, zigzagged — for her to make holes along. Offer help if she needs it and praise all of her efforts.

6. USING A PEN

Age Range
18-24 months

Materials
• Cardboard egg cartons or paper plates
• 2 pens

Whenever you set up an activity with writing utensils, do not leave your toddler alone with them. At this age her curiosity could lead her to poke a pen or sharp pencil into her ear or some other body opening. And she will almost surely be tempted to write on your walls or furniture. If you have some thin cardboard egg cartons, you can try the following safe pen activity with your child. It will challenge her eye-hand coordination skills.

Show your toddler an egg carton and poke some holes in it with a pen. Then invite her to poke a few holes. Let her hold the pen however she wants — either whole-fisted or overhand. She may want to concentrate on poking holes at random for a while.

Use a new carton or plate and mark a small circle on it with your pen. Ask your child to poke a hole in your circle. If she can't hit the target, hold her hand and help her. Make some other circles for her to spear. Then draw a line and show her how to poke holes along it. Make other lines —

7. LOTTO

Age Range
24-30 months

Materials
- Several sheets of construction paper
- Scissors, pen, and ruler
- Booklet containing several pages of gum-backed pictures (available in toy or variety stores)

Lotto is a simple table game that requires your child to match similar or identical pictures. Although simple, it challenges important visual skills (visual identification), cognitive skills (memory, categorizing, and matching), and physical skills (eye-hand coordination).

First, make a lotto master card for your toddler by dividing a sheet of construction paper into eight spaces:

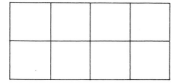

Stick a different picture on each section of the card. Then cut out eight squares of paper the same size as those on the master card. For each picture on the master card, stick an identical picture on a paper square.

Put the squares in a stack and place them facedown on the floor or a table. Put the master card in front of your child. Help him become acquainted with the pictures on the card by pointing to each one and asking him to label it or repeat the name after you.

Then turn over one picture square and ask your toddler to name the picture. Point to the master card and ask, **"Do you see another bird on this card?"** If he doesn't respond, hold the picture square next to the identical picture on the master card. **"Here's another bird. See, this is a bird and this is a bird, too."** Tell him to put the picture square on top of the identical picture on the master card. Continue with the other picture squares, encouraging your child to do as much as possible by himself.

A homemade lotto card with 10 spaces.

8. WORKING WITH CLAY

Age Range
24-30 months

Materials
- Playdough or homemade clay (see below)
- Butter knife, buttons, cookie cutters, pipe cleaners, cups, rolling pin, and plastic tumbler (optional)

Clay is a great material for toddlers to work with. It has a delightful feel, and a child can change its shape easily. At this age your toddler will spend her time merely manipulating the clay. As she gets older, she will make creations with it. Provide soft clay for her to use — preferably playdough or homemade clay. To make clay, combine

> 2 cups baking soda
> 1 cup cornstarch
> 1 1/2 cups *cold* water.

Bring the mixture to a boil, stirring constantly. Cook until the mixture has the consistency of mashed potatoes. (For variety, add a few drops of food coloring.) Remove the mixture from the pan and cover it with a damp cloth. Cover your clay with plastic wrap and store it in the refrigerator.

Toddlers love to pound!

Use some of the following suggestions to help your child have fun playing with clay.

- Roll a ball of clay for each of you. Show her how to squeeze it in her fist. If she squeezes very tight, it will squish between her fingers.

- Demonstrate how to pound the clay until it is flat. Have your toddler feel the flattened clay. **"This clay feels so** *smooth.* **It's flat like a pancake."**

- Show her how to roll pieces of clay on the table to make snakes. If she needs help, hold her hand and roll with her. Attach the ends of a snake to make a bracelet for your toddler.

- Give your child a butter knife and show her how to cut one snake into little snakes.

- Give her large buttons, cookie cutters, pipe cleaners, cups, and other decorative things to push into the clay.

- Show your child how to flatten the clay with a rolling pin or large plastic tumbler. 🧍

9. HIDE-AND-SEEK

Age Range
24-30 months

Materials
- Teddy bear or doll

Hide-and-seek is a traditional favorite that is sure to please your two-year-old. But since his attention span is still very short, you will need to play a simplified version of the game. Use a favorite teddy bear or doll to add something special to the game.

Have the doll or teddy say hello to your child and chat a while. Then suggest that the three of you play a game together. Explain the game briefly: **"You close your eyes. Then teddy will hide somewhere, and you can find him!"**

Chances are, it will take several trial runs before your child understands the rules. So tell him to close his eyes. Then while you go to the hiding place, keep reminding him to keep them shut: **"Keep your eyes closed. Close them tight."** Hide the bear somewhere close and very obvious, letting some of it show. Then say, **"Open your eyes and find teddy! Where is he?"** If he doesn't find it immediately, give clues or jiggle the teddy bear to attract his attention.

Play several rounds of the game and then let your child have a chance to hide with teddy. He will probably return to the same spots you chose. Act surprised when you find him and tell him what a good game player he is.

10. USING PROPS TO ACT OUT A STORY

Age Range
24-30 months

Materials
• Doll or stuffed toy
• Toy telephone, bowl and spoon, bar of soap, hand towel, toothbrush, comb (or props of your choice)

Listening to simple stories is probably one of your child's favorite activities. Add to the fun by inviting her to act out a story that you tell. Tell her the following story (or one of your choice) and use the corresponding props to portray each action:

• Yolanda's grandmother called her on the telephone and invited her to go to the zoo. First Yolanda must get ready.
• She eats a bowl of soup for lunch.
• Then she washes her hands with soap.
• She dries her hands with a towel.
• She brushes her teeth.
• And she combs her hair.
• She waves good-bye to her family. Yolanda and her grandmother will have a wonderful time at the zoo.

Retell the story several times. Ask your toddler to use the props and repeat the actions after you. When she is very familiar with the story, encourage her to do the actions without watching you first. If she needs help, hand her the correct prop as you describe the action and encourage her to use it. Eventually she will enjoy

choosing and using the props by herself as you tell the story.

For variety, pantomime the actions instead of using props.

Acting out a story about going to the store.

11. ANIMAL SOUNDS

Age Range
24-30 months

Materials
• Magazine pictures of animals
• Scissors
• Popsicle sticks (optional)

Is your toddler fascinated with animals? Most young children have at least one animal name in their list of first spoken words. And many toddlers are delighted by a visit to a petting farm. As you cut pictures from magazines for this activity, choose animals that make distinctive sounds, such as a dog, cat, horse, cow, frog, owl, donkey, and turkey.

Place the animal pictures in a stack and look at them one at a time with your child. Name each animal and make its sound. Then ask him to make the sound, too: **"That's a donkey. 'Hee-haw,' says the** donkey. You say 'Hee-haw.'" Praise your toddler for any attempts he makes at the sound. Some of them might be hard for him to make.

Look at the pictures again. Before you show your child each animal, tell him what sound it makes and ask him to tell you what animal it is: **"The next animal says 'Meow.' What is it? Right! It's a cat. See the cat."** At first, he might need a bit of coaching. But after you look through the pictures several times, he'll be able to identify most of them without any help.

For variety, you might paste a popsicle stick to the back of each picture. When you show the picture, you can move it around as you would a puppet. Toddlers love to watch!

word or two of your own message, or she may only breathe heavily in your ear. When she is finished, thank her for her message.

12. WHISPERING

Age Range
24-30 months

Materials
- None

Once in a while, share a whisper with your two-year-old. She will be tickled with the change in your voice! Whispering is a good activity for quiet times of the day, such as just before bed. And since whispers are secretive and giggly and very "touchy," they can easily lead to loving hugs.

Make a big deal out of your whispering: **"(Child's name), I've got a big secret to tell you. Come close so I can whisper in your ear. Now sit very still while I tell you."** Your message might be newsy ("We're going to the beach today") or a tender message ("You're my little sweetheart").

Invite your child to whisper something back to you. She might merely repeat a

13. STRETCHING

Age Range
30-36 months

Materials
- 2 pieces of elastic: one 24" long, the other 18" long
- Safety pins

With a little imagination, just about anything can become a toy. If you have two pieces of elastic, you and your child can play a game of "I'm Stretching."

Pin (or sew) together the ends of each elastic piece so that you have two circles of elastic. Step into the large circle and pull the elastic up around your ankles. Hold your feet apart until the elastic stretches, and say, **"Look at me. I'm stretching!"** Help your toddler put the other piece of elastic around his ankles. Then encourage him to spread his legs like you: **"Can you do this, too? Stand like me."**

Ask your child to copy other positions with the elastic around his ankles. You might stand on your hands and feet, stand up and jump forward once, stretch one foot forward or backward, or lift one leg up. (Be prepared for a few tumbles!) Encourage him to make up movements for the two of you to do.

14. SQUEEZE A COLOR/SQUIRT A PICTURE

Age Range
30-36 months

Materials
- Eyedropper
- Food coloring
- 3 baby-food jars
- Newspaper and paper to paint on
- Protective clothing

The word *painting* often brings to mind a picture of a person standing in front of an easel with a paintbrush in hand. You may not feel ready to arm your toddler with a paintbrush, but keep in mind that painting can be done with fingers, cotton swabs, pussywillows, potatoes, straws, and even eyedroppers. Squeezing an eyedropper is a good way to develop small-muscle coordination. Painting gives your child an opportunity to be creative and to learn about colors.

To prepare the activity, cover a work surface with newspaper. Put 1/2" to 1" of water in each baby-food jar and add a different color of food coloring to each jar. Place the eyedropper, paper, and baby-food jars on the newspaper and you're ready to invite your toddler to paint (if she hasn't already invited herself): **"You can use these things to paint a picture."**

Begin, **"This is an eyedropper. There is colored water in these jars. This is red, this is blue, and this is yellow."** Show your child how to pick up the eyedropper and how to squeeze the bulb: **"The eyedropper is empty. Put it into the water in one of the jars and let go of the bulb. Now take the eyedropper out but don't squeeze the top. Look, there is colored water in it! Hold the**

Finger-painting can be great fun.

49

eyedropper over the paper and squeeze the top again. The water is going onto the paper. There is red on the paper and the eyedropper is empty again."

Let your toddler continue painting in this manner. It may take a while for her to know when to squeeze and when to let go, so stay nearby to give her a hand or a reminder when she needs it. Call attention to the colors she is using and to what happens when two colors mix (for example, yellow and blue make green; red and yellow make orange).

15. STATUES

Age Range
30-36 months

Materials
• Record player or radio

Playing "Statues" encourages a child to move freely to music. It can be played inside, so it's a good activity for a rainy day. Because it takes very little preparation, it answers the question "What can I do now?"

Begin by saying, **"I'm going to show you how to play a new game. It is called 'Statues.' I'll play some music for you to dance to. When I stop the music, you stop dancing."** Show your child how the game is played so he can see some of the unusual positions he can be caught in when the music stops. Since it is difficult to demonstrate with a radio or record player, hum a tune. When you stop humming, also stop moving. You may be caught with your arms over your head, bending over, or in the middle of a sway. When your child seems to understand, let him try the activity.

It is fun to play "Statues" with several people since each person will end up in a different position. Try the activity with others or when your toddler has some friends over for a party.

If you put on paper-bag costumes, you and your toddler can become robots instead of statues.

16. FUN WITH A FLASHLIGHT

Age Range
30-36 months

Materials
• Flashlight

Playing with a flashlight will help to brighten up some dull moments on a wintry or rainy day. It can also be used to sharpen your child's vocabulary and memory.

Show your child the flashlight. Demonstrate how to turn the switch on and off and let her try turning it on and off by herself. With the flashlight in one hand and your toddler's hand in the other, go to her room. Explain, **"We are going to play a game with the flashlight. We can see the flashlight best if it is dark, so I'm going to close the curtains."** Do so, and then turn on the flashlight, briefly shining it on different objects in your child's room. **"This is a dancing light. It likes to move all around, but once in a while it needs to rest. When the light stops, you tell me what it is shining on."** Once she has named the object, bounce the light around and then shine it on something else. Continue as long as she is interested. Give her a turn at shining the light on objects that you then identify.

The activity is more challenging than it may seem since the light may shine on only part of an object. It may shine on one drawer of the dresser or a leg of a chair. Your child will have to identify the object after seeing only a part of it.

A flashlight can also be used to challenge your toddler's memory. Ask her to look around a room of your house for a few moments to see where things are in the room. Then darken the room and give her the flashlight. Name an object in the room and ask her to show you where it is by shining the flashlight on it. Start by naming obvious things such as large pieces of furniture. If she doesn't have any trouble remembering where the furniture is, name smaller items such as a picture, magazine rack, or light switch.

17. PAINT-STAMPING

Age Range
30-36 months

Materials
- Pot-pie pan or margarine tub
- Newspaper, paper towels, and white paper
- Assorted fruits and vegetables cut in half: green pepper, carrot, celery, potato, orange, lemon, apple
- Assorted kitchen items: corks, cookie cutter, forks
- Tempera paint
- Protective clothing

Does the thought of your child painting bring to mind a picture of a huge mess and therefore something to be avoided at all costs? A toddler painting activity does not have to be a disaster! In fact, with careful preparation and supervision, it can be a great learning experience and a lot of fun. Your child will be very proud of the work of art he creates, and so will you.

Stamping with a wooden block.

To prepare for painting, cover a work surface with newspaper. For added peace of mind, your child can work outside on the sidewalk or driveway. Fold two paper towels and put them in the pot-pie pan;

then add paint to soak the towels. Place the pan and a white sheet of paper in the center of the newspaper. Place the fruits, vegetables, and utensils (to be used for printing) next to the paint.

Say to your toddler, **"I have something special for you to do today. You can make a pretty design on this paper using the paint and these things."** Hold up each item and ask him to tell you its name. Tell him the color of the paint. Then explain, **"Watch how I make a design with the orange. First I dip it into the paint. Then I press the painted side onto the paper. Look at what happened! Isn't it pretty? Now you choose something to make a design with."**

Encourage your child to make a design, giving help if necessary. Be sure to compliment him. He may want to use the same item over and over again, or he may try each item once and then return to his favorite. If he fills one sheet of paper with designs and is still interested in printing, give him a second sheet. When he is finished, ask him to help with at least one part of the cleanup, such as throwing the newspaper into the trash.

On the Move

1. Climbing
2. Walking Up Stairs
3. On, Off, and In
4. Walking Backwards
5. Caterpillar Parade
6. Walking Down Stairs
7. Obstacle Course (Part 1)
8. Jumping Off a Step
9. Somersaulting
10. Walking the Plank
11. Playing a Ball Game with a Playmate
12. Climbing Around on a Ladder
13. Obstacle Course (Part 2)
14. Throwing On-Target
15. Walking Like the Animals
16. Chasing Bubbles and Balloons
17. Jungle Walk
18. Batting a Ball

1. CLIMBING

Age Range
18-24 months

Materials
- Sturdy cardboard cartons
- Old tires
- Inflated inner tubes

Introduce your child to a new adventure by putting together a simple homemade climbing apparatus. Climbing is an important toddler activity that develops muscle coordination.

Arrange the climbing materials on a grassy area or in a carpeted playroom where bumps and falls won't hurt too much. Place a carton open side up for your toddler to climb into. Put several large and small boxes upside down for him* to climb into and over. Cut the bottom out of a large carton and set it on its side for him to crawl through. Pile the tires in a mound for him to climb on and jump off.

Climbing is an important toddler activity.

Show your toddler each item and encourage him to give it a try. If he is a climber, he won't need any coaxing. But if he seems hesitant, have him hold your hand while he climbs up the mound of tires, or stand nearby to give him confidence as he goes over, into, and through the boxes. Talk to him encouragingly: **"Come through this box and give me a hug. That's it, you can crawl right through it."**

Once your child feels sure of himself, urge him to move around on the objects without your help. If he becomes involved with the apparatus, he will probably rearrange objects to suit his own climbing tastes.

2. WALKING UP STAIRS

Age Range
18-24 months

Materials
- None

Stairs have probably fascinated your child since she* was crawling. Now that she walks skillfully, she is ready to begin walking up stairs while holding your hand. Stairs are a great challenge for your child, but they may also scare her. This activity will help her enjoy her first attempts at walking up stairs.

Before you begin, sit on the bottom stair and tell her, **"I am going to sing a song about a bear and a mountain. You will be the bear in my song, and these stairs will be the mountain."** Then sing a verse of "The Bear Went Over the Mountain":

The bear went over the mountain.
The bear went over the mountain.
The bear went over the mountain
To see what she could see.

---

*In odd-numbered activities, the toddler is referred to as a boy. In even-numbered activities, the toddler is referred to as a girl.

*In even-numbered activities, the toddler is referred to as a girl. In odd-numbered activities, the toddler is referred to as a boy.

Stand with your child at the bottom of the stairs and have her take your hand. Tell her to put her other hand on the railing. Say, **"Now I will sing 'The Bear Went Over the Mountain' again, and we will walk up these mountain stairs."** Her confidence on stairs is probably good if you have stairs in your home. But if she rarely gets a chance to crawl up and down stairs, she may need extra help as she walks up. While you help her go up, keep in mind that she is too young to alternate her feet on the steps. She will stop on each step and use the same foot to step up each time.

Offer a helping hand and stay by your child's side.

After you go up two or three steps, let your child crawl down in her usual way. Then invite her to walk up with you again. Be

prepared to repeat! If she enjoys this activity, she will want to continue much longer than you will. ✖

3. ON, OFF, AND IN

Age Range
18-24 months

Materials
- Sturdy cardboard box large enough for toddler to sit in

For your toddler, learning is most fun when he can move around. Take advantage of such moments by teaching him the concepts *on, off,* and *in.* He will get a chance to climb all over a box while he's busy following your directions.

Fold the flaps on the open end of the box toward the inside. Then lay the box on its side. Invite your child to climb on the box: **"Climb on the box, (child's name). Here** (point), **this is *on* the box."** Repeat the word *on* several times. **"You're on the box. I see you on the box."**

Next, tell your toddler to climb *off* the box. Again show him where to go if he doesn't understand you. Ask him to climb on and off several times until he seems very familiar with these two words. Applaud and cheer as he follows your commands.

Then invite him to go *in* the box. Play a game of "On, Off, and In" until he can follow your directions easily. ✖

4. WALKING BACKWARDS

Age Range
18-24 months

Materials
• Toy tow truck, or picture of tow truck

Your toddler may enjoy the challenge of walking backwards, but you will probably need to help her at first since walking backwards requires good balance. If you add a bit of imagination to the task, she can become a big tow truck pulling a car.

Show your child a picture or a toy truck, and talk about it: **"This tow truck will pull a car to a garage. Then someone can fix the car."** If you have a toy truck, demonstrate how it pulls a car.

Next, invite your child to be a car while you pretend to be a tow truck. Stand facing her and hold her hands. Talk about how you will pull the car: **"You're a broken car and**

I'm a tow truck. I'll pull you to the garage."** Then walk backwards hand in hand with your child. She will be walking forward. Stop at a chair or table and announce, **"Here we are at the garage."**

Switch roles with your toddler: **"Now you be the tow truck and pull me to the garage."** Let her walk backwards very slowly until she is sure of herself.

Once your toddler is able to walk backwards confidently, tie a string around your waist as a "tow rope." Tell her to hold the rope and pull you toward her. She may not even realize that she is walking backwards all by herself.

Giving mom a tow.

5. CATERPILLAR PARADE

Age Range
18-24 months

Materials
• Picture of a caterpillar, or caterpillar puppet

Your child isn't quite ready to play cooperatively with other children (by sharing materials, following the same rules together, exchanging ideas), but young toddlers can get along while doing one activity at the same time. This caterpillar game is a way to encourage young children to play as a group. So when your toddler has company, show them how to be a caterpillar.

If you can find a puppet or a picture of a caterpillar, show it to the youngsters. Tell them that it has a long body and moves slowly along the ground. Ask them to say the word *caterpillar*. Then ask if they would like to be a long, wiggly caterpillar. If anyone refuses, let him watch. He might want to join after the fun begins.

Arrange the children so that they are standing in single file. Tell each one to hold on to the shoulders of the person in front of him. You will probably need to show each child where to put his hands. Then stand at the front of the line and place the lead child's hands on your waist. Say to the group, **"Here we are — a long caterpillar. Let's move around. Everyone hold on!"** Move slowly through several rooms of your house, pausing every once in a while to ask the children to name the room and various objects.

6. WALKING DOWN STAIRS

Age Range
18-24 months

Materials
• None

Walking down stairs can be a difficult feat for your toddler. Not only is it hard for her to keep her balance while stepping down, but often the stairs are very tall compared with her. Imagine walking down stairs that come to your knees! If you help your toddler learn this skill a "step" at a time, she will be doing it alone before long.

Start with the bottom stair or a stoop. Tell your child to walk up the stair alone. Then help her turn around to come down. Face her and have her hold both of your hands as she steps down. Remember to offer lots of encouragement and praise: **"Down you go. Look at that — all by yourself!"** When she seems confident with one stair, tell her to try two stairs. For the next few weeks, help her practice whenever you go down a stairway together. Let her creep down as she normally does until she reaches the last two stairs. Then help her stand up and walk down these two steps.

A toddler who's experienced at walking down stairs — with dad.

When your toddler is willing to walk down three or four stairs, stand next to her and have her hold your hand. Show her how to hold on to the railing with her other hand. Eventually, after lots of practice, let go of her hand. She may appreciate an encouraging countdown as she goes: **"Down-one, down-two, down-three, down-four . . . hurray!"**

7. OBSTACLE COURSE (PART 1)

Age Range
24-30 months

Materials
• Ball of twine or string

On a rainy or wintry day when your toddler is very restless, set up an obstacle path in your house. He will be able to channel some of his energy without destroying your household — and he'll be practicing important motor-coordination skills and learning key words.

Mark a path through several rooms of your house with the string. You might lay the string around a sofa, under a table, over the seat of a sturdy chair, up a stairway, and over a pillow on the floor.

Ask your child to follow you along the string path. Whenever you come to an obstacle, use the proper position word to describe your movements: **"Here's a big chair. I'm going to walk *around* it. You walk *around* it, too. *Around* the chair you go!"**

After you and your toddler finish the course, invite him to do it again. This time let him lead the way. Urge him along with praise and enthusiasm: **"There you go *over* the chair. You're a good climber!"**

8. JUMPING OFF A STEP

Age Range
24-30 months

Materials
• Piece of rope or string

There is something very thrilling about jumping off things. Although your toddler probably isn't ready to jump from "great heights," she will love the challenge of jumping off a door stoop or a bottom step. Using a piece of rope or string, you can create a game to play with your jumping toddler.

Chances are, your child already jumps off the bottom step when she walks down the stairs. If you haven't seen her do this, show her how before you begin the game. Tell her to stand on the last step. Then face her and have her hold your hands. Ask her to jump down. Have her practice jumping several times until she can do it alone.

To play the game, use the rope to make a line on the ground that is parallel to the step and about 3" away. Then stand on the step and jump over the rope as you say, **"Jump! I jumped over the rope."** Let your child have a turn. If she can jump over the rope easily, place it about 4" from the step. Take turns jumping with her as long as she is interested.

Two chairs plus one large box can make a challenging obstacle course.

Add variety to the jumping game by making a circle with the rope. Say **"Jump!"** as you jump into the circle from the step. You might also make other shapes to jump into: for example, a triangle, square, or diamond.

Be sure to emphasize to your toddler that she should jump only from the last step, never from anything higher. 🏃

9. SOMERSAULTING

Age Range
24-30 months

Materials
• None

Your child is constantly discovering new ways to move his body and to coordinate movements. By now he can probably run, walk up and down stairs alone, climb on furniture, and jump off low elevations. Another movement that you can teach your two-year-old is a somersault. He will be thrilled to learn this "big kid" stunt.

If the weather is nice, do this activity outdoors on a grassy area. If you must stay indoors, find a roomy area that is carpeted or padded. You might have an old mattress or piece of foam rubber that your child can do his tumbling on.

Demonstrate a somersault for your child. Start from a squat and make sure that you tuck your chin toward your chest when you roll; this will prevent neck or back injuries. After you roll, invite him to do it, too. Show him how to squat and place his hands on the floor in front of him, ready to roll. Then gently push his head down toward the floor while you push his bottom forward and over. Make sure that your child doesn't straighten his neck, for he might wrench it or flop over onto his back.

Practice the roll with your toddler until he can do it easily. If he becomes frustrated, stop for the time being and try it again in a few weeks. When he does try the somersault alone, make sure that he always tucks his chin to his chest. And whenever he rolls, cheer him on: **"There you go — rolling like a ball. Yeah!"** 🏃

10. WALKING THE PLANK

Age Range
24-30 months

Materials
• Plank about 4' long and 1' wide
• Sturdy, low stool
• Ball

Your two-year-old is probably becoming more and more sure of herself on her feet. She likes to walk, run, jump, and climb, and she may seem to be in perpetual motion. Although watching your toddler may be enough to wear you out, remember that she needs to practice these large-motor skills in order to perfect them.

Set the plank on an incline with one end resting on the stool and the other end on the floor. Then invite your child to walk the plank. She will probably want to hold your hand as she moves along. If she doesn't want help, stand close by so that you can catch her if she slips off.

When your child reaches the top, reward her with the ball. She may want to toss it back to you, roll it down the plank, or simply throw it. Then help her turn around and walk back down the plank. Let her practice walking the plank as long as she's interested.

To vary the activity, invite your child to "walk" the plank in different ways — for example, by crawling or sliding. She might

Offer a helping hand to steady your toddler.

love to pretend to be a little monkey crawling up a tree branch.

As another variation, your toddler might like to play with the ball. She can roll it up the plank, stand by the side and roll it down, or make up other games. 🌟

11. PLAYING A BALL GAME WITH A PLAYMATE

Age Range
24-30 months

Materials
• Tennis-size ball
• Blanket or large towel

Playing games with other children requires cooperation, but keep in mind that cooperating is a tough thing for a two-year-old to do. When your child has a friend to play with, teach them a ball game that helps make cooperating fun. To play this game, they will need to work together and share the playthings.

Spread the blanket on the floor or grass and place the ball on it. Ask your child to stand along one side of the blanket. Have his playmate stand along the opposite side. The two players should be facing each other. Tell them to bend down and grab the corners of the blanket. If they don't understand your directions, demonstrate what to do.

Then tell the players to lift the blanket carefully so that the ball doesn't roll off. If they don't lift the corners of the blanket together, they will lose the ball. Then tell them to raise and lower the blanket so that the ball bounces up and down. Encourage them to keep the ball on the blanket, but don't interfere. Let them solve this problem together. Of course, they might change the rules of the game, but that's okay! If this activity seems to be beyond their abilities, wait a few weeks and try it again. 🌟

12. CLIMBING AROUND ON A LADDER

Age Range
24-30 months

Materials
• Ladder
• Chair

If you have a ladder in your garage or tool shed, use it to encourage your toddler to do some climbing. Besides getting exercise, she will learn more about her body and how to move it.

Lay the ladder flat on the floor or ground. Demonstrate how to step *between* the rungs. When your toddler masters this movement, challenge her to walk *on* the rungs. Have her hold your hand if she is unsteady. You might also show her how to jump *over* the rungs, walk on her hands and feet *between* the rungs, and walk on her hands and feet *on* the rungs. All of these activities promote motor coordination, along with eye-hand and eye-foot coordination. Emphasize the position words as you describe and demonstrate the actions.

Stepping between the rungs of a ladder.

Next, hold the ladder on its side and encourage your child to crawl back and forth between the rungs. While you hold it, she might also crawl over the ladder, climb on the ladder and straddle the side beam, and scoot forward and backward while straddling the side beam.

For more advanced play, prop one end of the ladder on a chair or other support. Demonstrate how to crawl up and down the ladder on your hands and feet. You might also have your toddler hold your hand as she walks up and down on the rungs of the ladder.

Be sure to remove the ladder when you're finished with the activity.

13. OBSTACLE COURSE (PART 2)

Age Range
30-36 months

Materials
• See below

Obstacle courses are fun and challenging for children of all ages. They are a great form of exercise, since they require children to move different muscles in a lot of different ways. But to a child, exercise is the last thing on his mind. He's concerned with conquering each obstacle in front of him. A feeling of great satisfaction accompanies the sense of challenge. In fact, the whole experience can be so rewarding he will do it again and again.

You can make an obstacle course with assorted materials; following is a list:

• *Boxes:* Your child can jump or step over small boxes, or crawl over or through large boxes. He can also push a large box.

• *Mattress, Blanket, or Sheet:* When one of these items is placed on the ground, your toddler can roll and tumble on it. A blanket or sheet draped over the back of two chairs forms a tunnel to crawl through.

• *Tires:* Your child can step or jump into and back out of a tire. Several tires in a row become even more challenging.

• *Chairs:* Chairs are good for climbing over and crawling under. A broom placed across the seats of two chairs is also good for crawling under. He can practice jumping or stepping over a string tied to two chair legs (2-3" off the ground).

• *Ladder:* Lay the ladder on the ground. Your toddler can step between the rungs or try to step only on the rungs. He can also jump over each rung.

• *Carpet Samples:* Lay a series of carpet samples in a row for your child to walk along or jump on.

• *Tape or Rope:* Place rope or tape on the floor in different patterns for your child to follow. Two parallel strips of tape or rope can make a straight or zigzag path for him to walk through. One strip can be a curved or straight path for him to follow. You can include one or two paths in your obstacle course or make a path between obstacles.

Pushing, climbing, jumping, and hopping!

If possible, put the obstacle course somewhere where you can leave it for a few days so that your child can have many chances to enjoy it. Once the course is set up, show him how to get past each obstacle. If he needs some help, hold him at his waist so his hands are free to use for balancing. Once he has mastered the course, you can change it or you can show him how to move through the same course in different ways. He can jump, walk backwards, walk sideways, take big steps, or take little steps on your command. 🏃

14. THROWING ON-TARGET

Age Range
30-36 months

Materials
• Bean bag
• 2 yards of rope
• Masking tape
• Laundry basket, or bucket (optional)
• 3 household objects (optional)
• 2 chairs, string (optional)

Most children can throw things fairly easily. But the problem for most children is to make things land where they want them to. Throwing objects at a target is a good way for your toddler to develop her aim as well as her arm muscles. By making the target smaller or the distance longer, you can ensure that the activity will remain challenging to her for years to come.

Bean bags are great for throwing at targets: they are easy to hold on to, they make a nice "thud" when they hit, and they don't roll away after they land. They are also easy to make. If your child doesn't have a bean bag, a pair of socks or a knotted towel will do. To set up the activity, make a circle on the floor with the rope. Place a strip of masking tape on the floor about 6' away from the circle.

Give your child the bean bag and ask her to throw it into the circle while standing behind the strip of masking tape. Once she hits the target with ease, you can vary the activity in a number of ways. You can make the circle smaller or move the masking tape farther away from the target. The rope circle can be replaced with a laundry basket or a bucket. You can also make more than one circle on the floor and then ask her to throw the bean bag into the circle you point to. Try placing a different object in each circle (for example, a wooden spoon, throw pillow, and stuffed animal). Then ask your child to throw the bean bag into the circle with the spoon.

Try placing two chairs 6' apart in front of the circles and tie a string to the legs of the chairs. Ask your toddler to throw the bean bag over the string and into the circle. Or tie the string to the top of the chairs and ask your child to throw the bean bag *under* the string. ✵

15. WALKING LIKE THE ANIMALS

Age Range
30-36 months

Materials
• None

Most children love animals. They like to cuddle toy animals and make sounds like real animals. This activity encourages your toddler to move the way animals move. Moving like animals will give him a chance to exercise his large muscles and use his imagination to become those animals. The activity can be done inside on a rainy day; your child can really take off if you do the activity outside.

There are lots of ways your toddler can move and lots of animals he can pretend to be. Demonstrate the following movements to him, each time naming the animal you are pretending to be. To make the animals seem more real, spice up the movements any way you like. He may not be able to do the movements correctly, but a good try is all that's needed for this activity. With a few months of growing and practice, his coordination will improve and the movements will come easier.

• Crawling on hands and knees (dog, cat)
• Crawling on stomach (snake, crocodile, alligator)
• Jumping forward (rabbit, kangaroo)

• Running with arms outstretched to the side (bird)
• Squatting while walking (duck)
• Squatting while hopping (frog)
• Leaping (deer)
• Walking slowly with hands clasped and hanging down in front (elephant)
• Running or galloping (horse)
• Walking slowly, bending at the waist, arms bent and hanging down at side (spider)
• Lying on stomach, kicking legs (fish, whale, porpoise)

Be sure to take part — this is also *your* chance to walk like the animals. ✵

16. CHASING BUBBLES AND BALLOONS

Age Range
30-36 months

Materials
• Bubble-blowing liquid and wand
• Balloons

Running is always a good way for a toddler to get exercise and to channel energy. Your child may not be too cooperative if you ask her to jog around the house several times, but chasing a balloon or bubbles may keep her running for quite a while. You may even find yourself drawn into the activity.

Bubbles can be purchased at most toy stores and discount stores. They can also be made by mixing 1/3 cup of liquid detergent with 2/3 cup of water. A wand can be made by bending a piece of wire, or you can use an empty spool. Blow the bubbles into the air. Ask your child to chase them and pop as many as she can before they reach the ground. She will probably want to take a turn at blowing bubbles. Give help as needed. The most difficult thing to learn about blowing bubbles is how hard to blow. It's something she will learn with practice.

Balloons are also fun to chase. Keep several on hand since there is always a chance the balloon will pop. Show your toddler how to toss the balloon into the air and how to bat it with her hand to keep it up. Teach her to hit it from underneath so that it stays up in the air. 🏃

17. JUNGLE WALK

Age Range
30-36 months

Materials
• Two 6' pieces of rope or heavy string
• Two 3' pieces of rope or heavy string
• Pictures of a jungle (optional)
• Hats (optional)

You don't need to travel to Africa to go on a safari. All you need is some rope or heavy string and some imagination. The surprises your child encounters during the safari will give him lots of practice developing large motor and eye-motor coordination. You can also take an opportunity to emphasize the words *on, over, under, in,* and *out.* Before beginning your walk, tie one end of a 6' rope to a door knob. Lay the other 6' rope on the floor in another part of the room. Lay the 3' ropes parallel to each other on the floor, 1' apart.

Introduce the activity to your toddler by telling him what a jungle is: **"Let's pretend to go on a walk through the jungle. A jungle is a hot place where lots of trees, bushes, and other plants grow. Monkeys, lions, and elephants live in jungles."** If you have some pictures of a jungle, show them to him as you describe it. **"I've never been in a jungle before, so I'm not exactly sure what it is like. But we'll probably find**

out during our pretend walk." If you like, you can wear hats to keep the hot sun off your face.

Begin walking around the room. Ham it up as much as you'd like. You can shade your eyes and talk as you walk: **"It sure is hot in the jungle** (fan yourself). **These bushes tickle my legs** (scratch your leg). **I think I hear a lion** (growl).**"** As you approach the rope tied to the door say, **"Look, there is a log across the path. I guess we will have to step *over* it."** Step over the rope. Then take the free end of the rope and raise it 1" off the ground for your child to step over. Drop the rope and walk through the room again.

As you walk, pretend to encounter other obstacles. The 3' lengths of rope can be a river for your toddler to jump over. If you move the ropes farther apart, they can become a path for him to walk on. Grab hold of the end of the rope tied to the door and raise it 1' off the ground. It can be a fence for him to crawl under. The fence can also be lowered to 6".

Jumping over a fence?

The 6' rope on the ground can turn into a snake to jump over (hold one end and wiggle it). You can also use the rope to make a lake. Jump into the lake, pretend to swim across, and jump out when you reach the other side. This same piece of rope can become a path when laid out straight on the floor. Straddle the rope and walk along it. If the jungle brush gets too heavy, you may have to bend over and walk on your hands and feet.

The whole family can take part in a ball game.

18. BATTING A BALL

Age Range
30-36 months

Materials
- Fly swatter, plastic bat, or Ping-Pong paddle
- Sheet of paper, whiffle ball, or sponge ball

Your child won't by ready for the major leagues after doing this activity, but she will know what it is like to hit a ball moving toward her. It's a skill that takes a lot of motor coordination. The more practice she gets at batting, the better she will become at it. She will be thrilled to see the ball fly through the air when she manages to make a hit.

Your toddler can practice batting with a fly swatter and a sheet of paper crumbled into a ball, with a plastic bat and a whiffle ball, or with a Ping-Pong paddle and a sponge ball. If she is using a plastic bat, show her how to hold it in both hands and stand with her side toward you. Then show her how to swing the bat forward. She will probably have a tendency to stand facing you and to swing the bat down. This makes it a lot harder to hit the ball. Occasionally remind her to get in the proper position.

If your child is using a fly swatter or Ping-Pong paddle, show her how to hold it in one hand. She should stand facing you and move the racquet forward and down to hit the ball. When she is all set with bat in hand, stand a few yards away from her. Throw the ball slowly so she has a chance to hit it. The first times she may swing too early, too late, too high, or too low. But occasionally the bat and ball will connect, and she will want to try again.

To make the game more fun, pretend the ball is a fly or bee. You can even draw or paste some eyes on it. Tell your child to swat the fly when it comes to her: **"Here comes a fly.** *Bzzz.* **Get it. Oops, it got past you. Here it comes again! Good, you got the fly!"**

Growing with the Grass

1. Pretending to Be an Animal
2. Whiffle Ball
3. Playing with Sand
4. The Slide
5. Listening to Language
6. Hide and Find in the Sand
7. Sandbox Roadway
8. Sorting
9. A Nature Walk
10. Repeating a Three-Word Sentence
11. Pouring from a Pitcher
12. Watching the Weather
13. Camping Out
14. Leaf Rubbings
15. A Walk in the Rain
16. Sand Pictures
17. Planting Seeds
18. Running

1. PRETENDING TO BE AN ANIMAL

Age Range
18-24 months

Materials
• None

Your child is just entering the age for make-believe. Right now it will be much easier for him* to imitate something if he can see it firsthand. Almost every neighborhood has some kind of animal life to look at — either pets, or wildlife, or farm animals. So take a walk in your neighborhood and look for some animals that your toddler can watch and then imitate.

As you walk, help your child look for animals. Dogs and cats are especially appealing to little ones, and they are easy to imitate. When you see an animal, name it and ask him to say the name, too. Then imitate the sound that the animal makes and urge him to repeat the sound: **"The dog says 'Woof-woof.' Say 'Woof-woof' like the dog. That's it! You sound like a dog!"**

Talk about something the animal is doing: **"Look at the dog run. She runs fast."** Then invite your child to do it, too: **"You be a dog, too. Run like her."** If he doesn't imitate the animal, show him how. Watch the animal together and talk about the things it is doing. Your toddler may copy a number of things the animal does. Give him lots of praise for his efforts.

When you are home, invite your child to be the animal again. If he can't remember what the animal does, model some movements for him to imitate.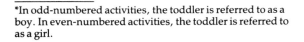

---

*In odd-numbered activities, the toddler is referred to as a boy. In even-numbered activities, the toddler is referred to as a girl.

A snow dog may give your toddler other ideas.

2. WHIFFLE BALL

Age Range
18-24 months

Materials
• Large plastic bat and whiffle ball
• Piece of rope about 3' long

Chances are, your child has seen someone use a bat to hit a ball. And if she* has, she would probably love to try it herself. She is still much too young to hit a pitched ball, but you can easily set up a beginner's game of "Swing and Hit."

---

*In even-numbered activities, the toddler is referred to as a girl. In odd-numbered activities, the toddler is referred to as a boy.

To set up the activity, tie one end of the rope to the whiffle ball. Then locate a tree that has a branch that hangs slightly above your child's head. If you don't have a tree like this in your yard, look for one at a local park, or you might use a clothesline or a beam in the roof of a carport or patio area. Tie the rope around the branch so that the ball hangs at your toddler's chest level.

Show your toddler how to hit the ball with the bat and then invite her to try it. Place her hands on the handle of the bat and help her swing a few times. Then let her do it alone. Offer lots of encouragement and praise, even if she misses the ball: **"Swing that bat. Good try, you almost hit it that time. Give it another swing."**

Several toddlers can have fun playing alongside one another.

3. PLAYING WITH SAND

Age Range
18-24 months

Materials
- Sandbox
- Cover: screen or canvas
- Playthings: pail, shovel, spoons, funnel, sifter, muffin tin
- Toys: cars and trucks, plastic people and animals, toy pots and pans

Now that your toddler has stopped putting everything into his mouth, he will enjoy playing with sand more than before. Besides having lots of fun, he will develop hand and finger coordination as he digs, pours, and stirs the sand. And if you talk to him while he plays, you can introduce such concepts as *empty, full, more, less, big,* and *little.* He may also begin to use his imagination to "cook" pretend sand meals, or dig a hole like a puppy, or move a toy car along sand roads.

If you don't live near a sandy beach or a park with a sandpile, try to provide a sandbox for your child. It doesn't have to be fancy — a large metal tub or a low plastic container will do fine. Try to supply a cover for the sandbox — neighborhood cats love to use sandboxes as litter boxes.

Over the coming weeks and months, you can watch your child use various sandbox toys more skillfully and with greater imagination. Let him have a lot of time to play alone in the sandbox. He will learn a great deal by exploring on his own. But he will also enjoy sharing some sandbox time with you. Provide a spoon or shovel for each of you and help him shovel sand into a pail or bowl. Emphasize words such as *empty, some, full, more, in,* and *out* as you work together: **"This pail is *empty*. Let's put *some* sand *in* it. Now there's sand *in* the pail."**

4. THE SLIDE

Age Range
18-24 months

Materials
• Ball

One of the most popular pieces of playground equipment is the slide. Slides are appealing to young children because they offer both a physical challenge and a thrilling ride. However, many young toddlers are afraid to climb the ladder or go down a slide alone. After all, it's a long way to the top and a long slide to the bottom. This slide activity offers your toddler an extra incentive for facing the slide by herself. But even if she doesn't need motivation to do it alone, she will enjoy this game.

For safety: Slides for toddlers should be 5' high or less; the steps should be flat, not rounded; there should be side rails on the ladder and slide bed; and the ground beneath the slide should be soft (grass or sand).

When the weather is nice, use a ball for this activity. If there is snow on the ground, roll a snowball and use it. Tell your child to watch as you hold the ball and climb the ladder on the slide. Then roll the ball down the slide and go down after it. Congratulate yourself and show lots of enthusiasm: **"Hurray for daddy! I rolled the ball down the slide."**

Invite your toddler to take a turn. Hold the ball for her while she climbs the ladder. As she goes up, emphasize the word *up:* **"You're going *up* the ladder. *Up* you go to the top."** If she is unsteady on the ladder, stand behind her as she climbs. In any case, stay at the bottom in case she slips and falls.

When your toddler reaches the top, hand her the ball and tell her to roll it down the slide. This time emphasize the word *down:* **"There it goes. *Down, down, down!"*** Encourage her to slide down after the ball. Stand by the side to reassure her: **"Go down and get the ball. There you go, all by yourself."**

Young children enjoy indoor slides, too.

5. LISTENING TO LANGUAGE

Age Range
18-24 months

Materials
• None

The best way to teach your toddler how to use language is to talk to him — not with baby talk or with nonstop chatter, but with everyday language that you use with everyone else. He won't understand everything you say, but he will get the general idea. And he needs to hear language over and over in order to learn how to use it himself. Talk to him while you're in the car together, or when you are giving him a bath, or while you're dressing him. Talk about what you are doing, where you're going, or what is on your mind. Another good time to talk to your child is when you are outdoors taking a walk together.

As you walk along, talk about the things that you see: **"There goes Eric on his new bike. He can ride it so fast."**

Pause occasionally to let your child add a word or two to the conversation if he wants. He might repeat a word or phrase that you said, or he might have something new for you to talk about. For example, if he sees a car and says "Car," talk about the car for a while: **"That car is making a lot of noise. It must need a new muffler."**

6. HIDE AND FIND IN THE SAND

Age Range
18-24 months

Materials
• Sandbox
• Small object: Ping-Pong ball or toy car

Sometime when your child is playing in the sand, join her for a sandy game of "Hide and Find." She'll practice cognitive skills and have fun at the same time.

Don't interrupt your toddler if she is deeply involved in play. But if she seems to be finished with her own sand games, sit down next to her and dig a hole. To catch her interest, talk about what you're doing: **"I'm making a hole to hide something in."** Then put an object into the hole and cover it with sand. **"My car's gone now. It's hiding under the sand. Where is it?"** If she doesn't try to dig up the car, dig for it yourself: **"Where is that car? Okay, car, you can stop hiding now. Where are you? . . . Here it is!"**

Hide the object again while your child watches, and then invite her to dig it out. If she needs help remembering where you buried it, make a circle around the area and

tell her to dig there: **"The car is hiding under this circle. Dig right here."** After she uncovers the object several times, she may want to bury it so that you can find it.

Finding a hidden toy.

7. SANDBOX ROADWAY

Age Range
24-30 months

Materials
- Sandbox
- Toy cars and trucks

Your child's sandbox play is probably becoming more sophisticated — more marked by make-believe and more imaginative. You can encourage his inventiveness by showing him how to transform a line in the sand into a road for his toy cars and trucks.

With your finger, make a line that has a 90° corner. Talk about this "road" and show your toddler how to move a vehicle on it: **"I made a long road to drive on. Look, this car is driving on the road. Now it's turning. Can you drive the car on the road, too?"**

Encourage him to keep the car on the line: **"Don't let your car go off the road — it will crash!"** Of course, crashing might become part of the game. **"Oh no! Your car had an accident. Put it back on the road and drive again."** Add curves and turns to the road to make it long and interesting.

8. SORTING

Age Range
24-30 months

Materials
- Paper bag

Human beings are natural organizers, and so your child will probably take to sorting tasks enthusiastically, even in early toddlerhood. The outdoors offers lots of things that your two-year-old can sort. When she sorts objects from nature, she must look at them carefully, compare them, and put them into categories. And so this task is an early introduction to the world of science.

Take a walk outdoors with your toddler. As you go, collect several samples of three different things. For example, you might find sticks, feathers, and dandelion flowers, or stones, acorns, and fallen leaves. Even in winter you can find a variety of samples.

After your walk, find an area outdoors where your child can sort her things. If you have a stairway with three or more steps, she can use that. A sidewalk with divided spaces is even better. Otherwise, you can draw three circles in a sandpile or make three circles with string on your driveway.

Empty the bag of treasures on the ground and name each object. Then place one type of thing in each divided area. **"Watch me, (child's name). I'll put a stone on this step, an acorn on this next step, and a leaf on the very top step."**

Hand your child an object from the pile and tell her to put it with the similar object: **"Here's another stone. Put it with the other stone."** Then hand her a different object and ask her to put it where it belongs. If she puts it in the wrong area, show her where it goes: **"The acorn goes here, with this acorn. Put your acorn here."** Hand her the rest of the objects one at a time. When she is finished, ask her to name each category. Then congratulate her on a job well done.

9. A NATURE WALK

Age Range
24-30 months

Materials
• None

Who doesn't love the outdoors? Even if you aren't a nature lover, you will probably enjoy a walk in the woods or a park with your toddler. The following suggestions can turn your walk into a learning adventure:

• Take only a 15-30 minute walk; otherwise, you might end up carrying a tired toddler. If he is still "rarin' to go" afterwards, make your next walk a little longer.

• Encourage your child to take a good look around him. Draw his attention to flowers, insects, tall trees, fallen branches, and logs on the ground. Name the things the two of you look at. You will probably discover a few things that are new to *you*. Even wintry woods can contain green mosses and protected plants, and winter is an excellent time to view birds' nests in the trees.

• Listen carefully together for animal sounds, the wind, running water, and the voices of other hikers. Name all the sounds you hear. You might also imitate animal sounds and ask your child to make the sounds, too.

• Encourage him to touch bark, rocks, flower petals, moss, wet surfaces, and other textured things. Describe the way things feel as he touches them: **"This rock is smooth. Oh! That part is bumpy."** Of course, learn to identify poisonous plants in your area and be alert for them on your walk.

• Use your nose! Almost everything in nature has some sort of odor. Ask your child if he likes the way different things smell.

Talk about your walk after you return home. Tell other family members about your hike, and ask your child to recall some things you both saw. If he doesn't name anything on his own, jog his memory: **"We saw a frog today. Say 'Frog.' And you especially liked the creek. Remember?"**

Be sure to stop and smell the flowers!

10. REPEATING A THREE-WORD SENTENCE

Age Range
24-30 months

Materials
• None

Language development knows no limitations of time or place — it can occur anytime or anyplace. The playground is a good place for encouraging your child to use sentences. When she wants something or needs help, model a sentence that she can use. Use simple three-word sentences that she can remember easily and then repeat.

If your toddler wants help in climbing onto a piece of playground equipment, teach her how to ask for help: **"Do you want to get on this merry-go-round? Say, 'I want up.' Then I'll help you get on."** Likewise, when she wants to get off, encourage her to say,

Now's the time to say, "Here I come!"

"I want down." If she uses only one word, such as *up,* say a complete sentence and prompt her to use it: **"Up? Oh, you want to get on. Say, 'I want up.' That's right! Here you go — up on the horse."**

Before you push your child on a swing, encourage her to ask: **"Do you want a push? Say, 'Push me high.'"** When she does say the sentence, reward her with a few pushes. Then encourage her to ask again. Once she catches on, asking for a push will become part of the fun of swinging.

11. POURING FROM A PITCHER

Age Range
24-30 months

Materials
• Small pitcher
• Spoon or sand shovel

Sandbox time is a good opportunity to introduce your child to pouring because sand acts much the same as water when it pours. So once he masters pouring sand in the sandbox, he can try pouring juice in the kitchen.

Before this activity, watch your child while he plays to determine if he has a hand preference yet. Many children do not show hand preference until they are three or older. If he does prefer one hand to the other, this is probably his dominant hand.

First, ask your toddler to help you dig a hole in the sand. Then shovel some sand into the pitcher, but don't fill it. Ask him to watch while you pour the sand from the pitcher into the hole. **"Watch this, (child's name). Watch me pour the sand into the hole. Do you want to try it?"** Shovel more sand into the pitcher and then place it near your child's dominant hand so that he can pour. If he needs help, hold his hand steady while he pours the sand.

To make the job more challenging, ask your toddler to pour sand from the pitcher into a very narrow hole. Once he becomes adept at pouring, have him pour into a container.

12. WATCHING THE WEATHER

Age Range
24-30 months

Materials
• Piece of fabric or crepe paper streamer

Observing the weather can be one of your child's first experiences in science. Although she is too young to understand why different weather conditions occur, you can teach her the names for various types of weather and explain what is happening in very simple language.

During any season of the year, look at the sky with your child and point out what you see: **"What a pretty sky! It's big and blue. See those clouds? They are white clouds. Can you say 'Clouds'? Where are the clouds? There they are — up in the sky."**

Conditions on a rainy or snowy day can be very dramatic, so there is a lot to see and talk about. If it is stormy outdoors, you will probably do your observing from a window. **"Look at all those dark clouds. The rain (snow) is falling from those clouds. Can you see the sun? It's hiding behind the clouds! Where are you, sun?"** If there are thunder and lightning, name them and explain that they are coming from the clouds, too. Talk about the rain or snow as it reaches the ground. Look for raindrops or snowflakes on the window, bushes, or other objects. Explain, **"The rain**

is water. It gives all the trees and bushes and grass and flowers a drink of water."

If you are watching snow, bring some indoors in a bowl and let your child watch it change to water: **"Look, the snow is melting. It's changing into water, because we brought it into our warm house."** Don't expect her to understand why the snow melts; it all seems like magic to her.

On a nice day, take your toddler's painting materials outdoors.

On a windy day, give your toddler a long piece of fabric or a streamer. **"The wind is making your paper move. It looks like it's dancing! The wind is blowing our hair and our clothes."** Point out other things that are moving in the wind: **"See those leaves? The wind is blowing them all over the ground."**

13. CAMPING OUT

Age Range
30-36 months

Materials
- Card table and sheet
- Tent, blankets, lawn chairs

You don't need to buy expensive camping equipment or travel a long distance to give your child the experience of sleeping under the stars. All you need are a few warm blankets and a patch of grass in your backyard. Your child will find sleeping outside quite a bit different from sleeping in a cozy bed. The ground is not quite as soft as his mattress; there is no need for a night light when the stars and moon are shining brightly; he'll hear sounds outside that he doesn't hear inside; and the air will feel cooler and crisper. But it won't matter when he has you by his side to snuggle up to.

Before camping *outside* you may want to camp *inside* with your toddler. A card table with a sheet draped over it can easily become a tent.

You can plan an evening under the stars in lots of ways. If you are planning a camping trip, this preview can be a good way to prepare your child for the trip. Try to make the experience as "real" as possible. If possible, set up a tent in your yard. Roast marshmallows and sing songs around a barbecue grill. Cook and eat breakfast outside the next morning.

If sleeping outside all night isn't your cup of tea, you can enjoy a modified version of camping out. If you don't want to sleep on the ground, get out two lawn chairs. You and your toddler can still roast marshmallows and enjoy the fresh air and the stars. After he has fallen asleep, you can carry him inside and tuck him in his bed. You can then slip into your own cozy, comfortable bed. Be sure to tell your child that you are going to take him inside once he is asleep so he won't be disappointed when he wakes up.

Whether you sleep in the open or under a tent, on the ground or on a lawn chair, your child will pick up on your enthusiasm. You can help him learn to enjoy and appreciate nature by enjoying and appreciating it yourself, even though it is in your backyard. ✖

14. LEAF RUBBINGS

Age Range
30-36 months

Materials
- Leaves
- Nontoxic paste, paper clips, crayons, 2 sheets of white paper
- Newspaper

Chances are, your child brings home many odds and ends that she has found outdoors. At times you may feel the best place for them is the garbage can. But to her they are treasures — and the garbage is hardly a fitting place for them. Rocks, for example, can be displayed in an empty egg carton. On the inside of the lid you can write down where and when she found them. A collection of leaves can be used for an art project. You can hang the picture on your child's wall or give it to some lucky person.

To make a leaf rubbing:

- Help your child put paste on the *edges* of the top side of a leaf. (The top side is the side without raised veins or stem.) Paste the leaf on a sheet of paper. Then help her paste several more leaves onto the paper. Be sure the edges are pasted down.

- Once the paste is dry, place the second sheet of paper over the leaves. Put a paper clip in each corner to hold the sheets of paper together.

- Remove the paper wrapper from a crayon. Show your toddler how to rub the side of the crayon over the covered leaves. The shape of the leaf will appear on the paper as she rubs.

Remove the paper wrapper from other crayons so your child can use a variety of colors. The crayon will probably go beyond the edge of the paper as she rubs, so you may want to put a sheet of newspaper underneath the white paper.

15. A WALK IN THE RAIN

Age Range
30-36 months

Materials
- Rainwear

Rainy days and kids often mix like oil and water. Your toddler may spend the day asking "What can I do now, Mommy?" or he may stare out the window with a look on his face as gloomy as the weather. A rainy day doesn't have to spell trouble. You can turn a rainy day into a special experience by taking a walk outside with him. Be sure it is not thundering or lightning on the day you take your walk. If you hear any thunder at all, even faintly in the distance, head home immediately. Dress your child in rain gear and clothes that will survive getting wet and maybe a little muddy.

Your toddler will enjoy feeling the rain against his hand. You may even find him sticking out his tongue, trying to catch a few drops of rain to taste. Point out how things look different when it's raining. The sky is brown or gray and you can't see the sun. Leaves and grass look shiny when

they are wet. The earth looks darker and feels softer. You can also mention some of the things you don't see because of the rain, such as birds, cats, squirrels, and butterflies. You may see a lot of worms on your walk which you wouldn't see on a sunny day.

Call your child's attention to the way the rain makes the air smell fresh. If a car passes by, you can talk about how the tires on a wet road sound different from tires on a dry road. You can also listen to the sound of the rain as it hits the ground, trees, and houses. Make your walk in the rain complete by splashing in a few puddles.

16. SAND PICTURES

Age Range
30-36 months

Materials
- Paper towels, sheets of paper, nontoxic glue, paper cups, plastic spoon, food coloring, sand, newspaper
- Salt, colored chalk, popcorn (optional)

You don't need crayons or paints to make a picture — pictures can be made with many things in many different ways. You can encourage creativity in your toddler by having her make pictures with a variety of materials. She can paint with pussywillows, print with vegetables, and make a collage out of seashells. She can also make pictures with sand!

Before turning the sand over to your young artist, it needs to be colored. She may enjoy watching you as you color it. Decide how many colors you want to make and fill paper cups halfway with sand. Put enough water in each cup to just cover the top of the sand. Put some food coloring in the cup and stir it with the spoon. Let the sand stand for 15 minutes in the food coloring. Pinch the side of the cup and pour out as much water as you can without losing the sand. Then pour the sand onto a paper towel and let it dry. Once the sand is dry, it is ready for picture-making.

To make cleanup easier, place a sheet of newspaper on the table. Put a sheet of white paper on top of the newspaper. Show your child how to make a design by squeezing or brushing glue onto the paper. You can also draw a simple picture on the paper and have her trace around the picture with glue. Give her the sand in paper cups and show her how to sprinkle or pour sand over the glue. Once the glue is dry, shake the extra sand from the paper and show her the creation.

A similar type of picture can be made with salt: stir a piece of colored chalk around in the salt to color it. Another time, try popcorn: Color the popcorn by dipping it into a glass of water mixed with food coloring. Quickly remove the popcorn and place it on a paper towel to dry. Draw a picture on a piece of paper or have your child draw one. She can fill in the picture by gluing on the popcorn.

17. PLANTING SEEDS

Age Range
30-36 months

Materials
• Seeds, spoon or trowel, soil

You probably won't have to ask your child twice to participate in this activity. It has two very appealing features — dirt and water. There is also something exciting and fulfilling about planting a seed, caring for it, and watching it grow. Caring for a plant is a good way to give your child a taste of responsibility. Once the activity is over,

you'll need lots of soap and water. Don't let the thought of dirt discourage you — many of the best learning experiences are a bit messy!

Potting plants is an indoor activity, too.

Purchase a package of seeds during a shopping trip with your child. Flowers will add beauty to the yard, and vegetables will add bounty to the dinner table. Ask him what he would like to plant. If you don't consider yourself one of those people with a green thumb, ask for advice at a local nursery. They'll be glad to tell you what plants you will most likely have success with. You can also pick up some books on gardening during a trip to the library.

Gather together the things you need for planting the seeds. Then read the directions to your child: **"It says these flowers need a lot of sunshine. Let's go outside and find a patch of ground that gets a lot of sunshine."** Continue by helping your child plant the seeds. He'll need to dig away some soil, place the seeds in the soil, cover them up, and water them. Talk about the care the seeds will need in order to grow: **"Seeds need lots of sunshine and water. The seeds will grow into pretty flowers."** Point out a nearby plant: **"Once that bush was just a seed and now it is a big plant. It will take some time, but someday the seeds you planted will grow into pretty flowers."** Show your child the picture of the flowers on the package the seeds came in.

Every few days make a point of going outside with your toddler to look at the seeds. The day you see something green poking through the soil will be very exciting. Keep track of the days it rains by having him make an X on a calendar. If three or four days go by without rain, it can be his job to water the seeds.

18. RUNNING

Age Range
30-36 months

Materials
• Soccer-size rubber ball

Your child's energy may seem never to run out. Although she may always be busy, she may not be getting the physical exercise she needs. Running is one of the best ways she can channel energy *and* get exercise at the same time. Running will also help her build up physical endurance. If she learns to enjoy physical activity now, it is more likely she will continue to enjoy it as she grows older.

Your toddler isn't ready yet for games with many rules, but she can play some simple running games. Here are a few suggestions:

• *Racing:* Short races are always a good way to exercise. Choose two markers in your yard or a park, such as two

trees, and challenge your child to a race. Begin at one marker and race her to the other one. Race again between the same markers or choose two new ones. If she enjoys being tickled, you can add some fun to the race by running behind her and "threatening" to tickle her if you catch her. Do so occasionally.

• *Kiddie-kick soccer:* You need to play this game on a baseball diamond, or set up an area with four bases. Slowly roll a rubber ball to your child as she stands at homeplate. Tell her to kick the ball and to run around the bases. If she hasn't run around bases before, you may need to run with her until she gets the hang of it.

• *Toddler tag:* Tag can be played with two or more people. Select two markers that aren't too far apart to use as bases. When someone is standing on base she or he cannot be tagged. But once off, that person is fair game for the person who is "it." When someone is tagged while off base, she or he becomes "it." Your child may need some reminding about the purpose of the bases. When chasing her you can remind her by saying, **"Run to the**

Playing a game of "Follow the Leader."

80

lawn chair — it is a base. Then I can't
tag you." When being chased by your
child, you can say, **"I'm on base now
so you can't tag me."**

A Classroom in the Kitchen

1. Stirring
2. Using Two-Word Phrases
3. Unwrapping a Surprise
4. Sorting Dishes
5. Exploring Water
6. Using a Fork
7. Clothespins
8. Unscrewing Lids
9. Setting the Table
10. Form Puzzles
11. Making Decisions
12. Outlining Objects
13. Short and Long
14. Spooning Beans
15. How Many?
16. Naming the Different One
17. Making a Meal
18. Identifying Foods by Taste

1. STIRRING

Age Range
18-24 months

Materials
- Bowl and spoon
- Various batters or liquids

Note: Any activity dealing with food should begin with proper hand washing.

Stirring is lots of fun, and it helps your child develop rhythm and coordination in his* arm muscles. However, a young toddler can make a colossal mess when he stirs liquid or batter in a bowl. If you want to stay calm while he's busy stirring, put the bowl in your kitchen sink where he can stir up a storm.

Stiff, heavy batters, such as cookie dough, are too difficult for a child to stir smoothly. He will only flip globs of batter out of the bowl as he tries to stir. Let him stir thinner mixtures, such as scrambled egg or french-toast batter, muffin or cake batter, or colored water.

Whipping up some soapy water!

---

*In odd-numbered activities, the toddler is referred to as a boy. In even-numbered activities, the toddler is referred to as a girl.

While your toddler stirs, talk about what he is doing and encourage him to talk, too: **"You're stirring the scrambled eggs. When you are finished, we can cook them. Say, 'Stir eggs.' Yes, you're stirring the eggs."**

2. USING TWO-WORD PHRASES

Age Range
18-24 months

Materials
- None

Take advantage of opportunities during the day to encourage your toddler to talk. Talk to her* often and respond when she talks to you. If she is saying single words now, as a next step encourage her to use two-word phrases. Mealtime offers a good opportunity for you to talk with your child and prompt her to talk back.

When you serve your child, use simple sentences to describe the food: **"Here are some carrot sticks for you to eat. They taste good, and they're crunchy."** Then urge her to describe the food, too, by asking questions and presenting two-word answers for her to repeat: **"Do you like the carrot? Say, 'Good carrot.' Yes, it is a good carrot."**

Serve small portions to your toddler and then encourage her to ask for more: **"Do you want more carrots? Say, 'More carrot.'"** Gradually teach her to use two words when she wants another serving. She will learn over time.

While you and your child are eating, talk to her about your day — what you did already

---

*In even-numbered activities, the toddler is referred to as a girl. In odd-numbered activities, the toddler is referred to as a boy.

that day, how you feel, the weather, something you want to do. If she contributes a word to the conversation, help her expand her statement: **"Ball? Oh, there's your red ball under the table. We were looking for that. Can you say 'Red ball'?"** 🧒🧒

What's inside?

3. UNWRAPPING A SURPRISE

Age Range
18-24 months

Materials
- Nutritious snack foods: salt-free cracker, rice cracker, graham cracker, dried fruit
- Wax or brown paper
- String, tape, nontoxic paste
- Box

Toddlers love to unwrap packages. It's great fun to rip apart wrapping to discover a surprise inside. You can provide your child with several enticing surprise snacks to unwrap while you are working in the kitchen. He will not only have a lot of fun, but also practice coordinating his eye and hand movements.

Wrap up several snack foods in wax or brown paper. Fasten each wrapping in a different way. You might twist the ends of one, tape another, loosely tie one package with string, and seal another one with paste. You might also put a surprise snack in a box and then wrap the box.

Hand your child one package at a time and tell him to open it: **"There's something good to eat in this package. Open it and see what's inside."** He will probably need little coaxing. But if he seems confused, begin to open it yourself to give him the idea. Then hand the package back to him and say, **"Now you do it. Finish opening this interesting package."** 🧒🧒

4. SORTING DISHES

Age Range
18-24 months

Materials
- Unbreakable dishware
- Large bowl
- 2 cookie sheets or plastic bowls
- Second set of unbreakable dishware (optional)

Sorting tasks are slightly more difficult for a child than simple matching games. When your toddler *matches* things, she has one or more models to look at and compare things with. When she *sorts* things, she must compare them with each other. Unbreakable dishware makes good sorting material for beginners. The sets of objects (cups, saucers, plates, bowls) are very different from each other, and the materials are easy for you to gather — they're as close as your kitchen cabinets. Toddlers respond to sorting tasks very differently — your child may be interested for only a short while or she may go through all your dishware before tiring of this game.

Begin with only two sets of objects for your toddler to sort, such as three saucers and three plates. Put these objects into a large bowl. She can use the cookie sheets or plastic bowls for sorting. If there is a double sink in your kitchen, she will enjoy sorting objects into the two sinks.

Put the two empty containers in front of your child and invite her to play with you. Hold up one object from the bowl and name it. Then ask her to name it, too: **"Here's a saucer. What is this? Say 'Saucer.'"** Then ask her to put it in one of the empty containers. Next, hold up the other kind of object from the bowl and name it. Ask her to put it in the second container. Then tell her to take another object from the bowl. Name it with her and ask her to put it with the identical object: **"What's that? Yes, it's a saucer. Put it with your other saucer."** Continue the procedure with the remaining objects. Offer less and less help as she gets the idea. Remember to praise her and let her know that you are having fun.

A more difficult feat: sorting silverware.

If your child enjoyed the sorting game, let her do it again with two different groups of dishware. This time, hand her the container of things and ask her to sort the objects by herself. ✖✖

5. EXPLORING WATER

Age Range
18-24 months

Materials
- Bath towel
- Large plastic bowl or tub
- Water toys: funnel, sponge, measuring cup, plastic bottles, toys
- Dish detergent and washcloth (optional)

Toddlers love water! And for good reason — water can pour, splash, and swirl 'round and 'round. Toy boats can float on water, while metal spoons sink right to the bottom. These are among the observations your child is busy making as he plays with water. When you are working in the kitchen you can set up a water tub on the floor that will keep him busy for quite a while.

Place a bath towel somewhere on the floor where you won't be working. Put a large plastic bowl or tub filled partway with water on the towel and place some water toys next to the container.

Let your child explore the water and toys freely while you work. From time to time, stop what you're doing and talk to him or play with him for a moment. You might put some toys in the water and make swirls

An older child will enjoy playing with a baster.

with your hand so that the toys float in circles. Invite him to do the same. Or you can swish the water and challenge him to grab one of the toys as it bobs up and down.

Show your toddler how to fill a funnel and hold it up so the water can run out. Introduce him to the concepts *full* and *empty*: **"This funnel is empty. There's no water in it. (Fill it) Now it's full of water. Uh-oh, the water's coming out. Where did it go?"**

If you are washing dishes, your child might want to do some washing, too. Squirt soap into his water and swish it around to make bubbles. Then hand him a washcloth. He may decide to wash his water toys in the soapy water or just play with the bubbles in his own way. **✷**

6. USING A FORK

Age Range
18-24 months

Materials
• Small metal fork with blunt tips
• Nutritious snack foods (see below)

Your toddler is probably eager to be just like the "big people" in her life. At mealtime she sees everyone else eating with forks, and she may already be trying to use one. But using a fork requires coordination and practice, so try turning *snacktime* into a lesson in fork handling.

Have your toddler use a small metal fork with blunt tips so that she won't spear herself. Choose snack foods that are soft, and cut them into fairly large pieces. You might serve cubes of cheese, cut peaches, bananas, pineapple, scrambled eggs, or small pieces of soft toast.

Help your child by holding your hand over hers as she spears the food and puts it into her mouth. She'll probably want to do it alone. Let her hold the fork with her entire fist or any other way she prefers. It may take several jabs before she can spear a piece of food. Remember to praise all her efforts: **"You're using the fork. You look just like a big girl."** **✷**

Spearing a peach slice.

7. CLOTHESPINS

Age Range
24-30 months

Materials
- 1-pound coffee can
- Nonspring clothespins
- Nontoxic paint in various colors

Your toddler probably enjoys doing tasks that seem very tedious to you. He might spend a long time putting buttons into a bottle or dropping stones into the cells of an egg carton. Perhaps he enjoys slipping hoops onto a pole. These activities might look boring, but they fascinate toddlers. As they play they coordinate eye and hand movements. They learn the concepts *empty* and *full*. And they enjoy the satisfaction of completing a task, no matter how simple it is. Fitting clothespins on the rim of a coffee can is a similar task that will keep your child occupied while you work in the kitchen.

Be sure there are no sharp pieces of metal on the rim of the can. (If there are, file them and tape the rim.) Show your child how to push a clothespin onto the rim. It may take some practice before he can do it himself. Once he gets the hang of it, ask him to put all the clothespins on the can.

If you paint the clothespins, the activity can also be an experience with colors. Begin with the primary colors — red, blue, and yellow. When your child picks up a clothespin, name the color for him: **"You have a *blue* clothespin. Can you place the *blue* clothespin on the can? Now there are two *blue* clothespins on the can."**

8. UNSCREWING LIDS

Age Range
24-30 months

Materials
- Unbreakable containers with screw-on lids: shampoo bottles, detergent bottles, jars
- Box with small toys: crayon, ball, toy animal

When you have kitchen chores to do, give your child this absorbing task of her own to work on.

Screw the lids loosely on the jars and set them on the floor. Put the box of toys next to the jars, and invite your toddler to sit with you near these things. Explain that you would like her to put the toys into the jars. Then demonstrate how to unscrew a lid from a jar and put a toy inside. **"I want to put these toys into the jars. First I have to take the lid off one jar, like this. Now I'll put a toy in it. There, one toy is in a jar. Now you put toys into these jars."**

Once your child has removed all the lids and put the toys into the jars, show her how to screw the lids back on. Place each lid on the matching jar and screw it slightly. Then ask her to make them tight. If she likes this task, she may repeat it several times while you are busy working. And she may make up her own variations on the activity.

9. SETTING THE TABLE

Age Range
24-30 months

Materials
• Paper placemats
• Clear contact paper

Your toddler is old enough to be a real help at mealtime, and setting the table can become his "official" job. With the help of a few homemade placemats you can expect your two-year-old to set the table by himself.

First, make a placemat for each person who sits at the table. To do so, draw a diagram of a table setting on a paper placemat. Then cover the placemat with clear contact paper so that you can wipe it off after every meal.

Setting the table with the help of a diagram.

Before a meal put a placemat on each place at the table. Then ask your toddler to help you set the table. Set one complete place setting at a time: plate, silverware, glass, napkin. As you match each piece of tableware to its place on the mat, talk about what you're doing: **"First, I'll put the plate on this big circle. See, this circle looks like the plate, so that's where the plate goes.**

This looks like the fork, so I'll put the fork here. . . ." Ask your child to put the pieces on the second placemat: **"Here's the spoon. Where does it go? Does it go here? No, that doesn't look like the spoon. This looks like the spoon. Put it here."**

Once your child catches on, let him set the table alone using the placemats as diagrams. After a few weeks ask him to set the table without the placemats. If he becomes confused, tape a placemat to the wall so that he can refer to it. 🧑

10. FORM PUZZLES

Age Range
24-30 months

Materials
• Form puzzle
• Clay or playdough
• Cookie cutters

Puzzles make excellent toys. Most children love the challenge of a puzzle that is appropriate for their skill level. While working a puzzle, toddlers coordinate eye and hand muscles and learn to look carefully and compare each piece with the puzzle frame.

If your child is unfamiliar with puzzles, begin with simple form puzzles. Form puzzles consist of individual pieces that fit into corresponding holes in a puzzle frame. You can buy your toddler a four- or five-piece form puzzle, or you can make her one by using clay or playdough and cookie cutters.

Simply roll out a large piece of clay until it is about 1/2" thick. Press four or five cookie cutters into the clay and lift out the forms. Show your child the clay puzzle frame and identify each form for her: **"Here's a star, and there's a circle."** Then hand her one form. Show her where it goes and ask her to put it in place. If she tries to force it in the wrong way, show her how to turn the form until it fits in the hole. Repeat this procedure with the other pieces.

When the puzzle is complete, help your child take the pieces out. Then ask her to work it all by herself. If she tries to put a form into the wrong space, tell her to look closely and find the correct hole: **"You have a bird in your hand. That hole looks like a star. Your bird doesn't go in that hole. Find the hole that looks like a bird."** If she becomes frustrated, point out the correct hole: **"Here it is! Your bird goes right here. Good job."** ✖

11. MAKING DECISIONS

Age Range
24-30 months

Materials
• Nutritious snack foods

Decisions are hard to make, especially for a two-year-old who doesn't quite understand the concept involved. You can help your child learn how to make decisions by offering him opportunities to do so. Snacktime is a good time of day for making decisions, especially if he already has definite opinions about what he likes to eat.

To avoid confusing your young child, expect him to make only one decision at each snacktime, and offer him only two choices: **"Would you like to eat applesauce or a banana?"** At first he may not understand what you are asking. Don't be surprised if he answers your question with a "yes." Show him his two choices and ask him to point to the one he wants. Then ask him to *tell* you: **"You pointed to the banana. Say, 'I want a banana.'"**

Once your toddler catches on to decision-making, carry it over to other times of the day — choosing what to wear, which toy to take outside, which book to look at. However, you will have to let him know when he does have a choice and when he doesn't. For example, if you tell him to lie down for a nap, he may decide that it's time to read books. In cases like this be firm. Let him know that it is time to take a nap. You might offer a choice within the limits of what is acceptable. For example: **"Would you like to get onto the bed yourself, or would you like me to help you?"** ✖

Choosing between two pieces of fruit.

91

12. OUTLINING OBJECTS

Age Range
30-36 months

Materials
- Jumbo crayons or washable marking pens
- Assorted containers: cans, margarine tubs, meat trays
- Paper

Your family probably goes through lots of disposable containers like metal cans, margarine tubs, yogurt and cottage-cheese containers, and styrofoam meat trays. To use this kitchen activity, save such containers over the next few days so that your child can trace around them on paper. She will be practicing important coordination skills.

Demonstrate to your toddler how to use one hand to hold an object steady on a piece of paper while you outline the object with the crayon or pen. When she tries it, help her hold the object steady as she works. When she becomes more familiar with the task, let her hold the object by herself as she outlines.

Your toddler will probably not follow the exact outline of the object. She may only trace the side near her writing hand and then scribble the rest. She may even change the activity and merely scribble around the object as it rests on the paper. Encourage her attempts at this challenging task.

13. SHORT AND LONG

Age Range
30-36 months

Materials
- Cooked spaghetti

This activity is for all spaghetti lovers. In it you use left-over spaghetti noodles to teach your child the meaning of the words *long* and *short*. To set it up, simply cut a noodle into fourths so you have four short noodles. You will also need two uncut (long) noodles.

On a table, place a short spaghetti noodle parallel to and just below a long one. Run your finger along the short noodle as you say, **"This noodle is short."** Run your finger over the long noodle saying, **"This noodle is long."** Then place the other noodles in front of your child and ask him to find another short noodle (point again to the short noodle in front of him). If he selects a long noodle, place it above the long noodle and say, **"This noodle is long. Can you find a short noodle like this other one?"**

After your child has found several short noodles and has placed them side by side, ask him to find a long noodle. Point to the long noodle to remind him what *long* looks like. Placing the long noodles side by side may require quite a reach, so be ready to help.

To add some suspense to the game, lay one short and one long noodle in front of your toddler. Curl the other noodles when you lay them down. Show him how to uncurl a noodle and lay it in a straight line to see if it is long or short.

14. SPOONING BEANS

Age Range
30-36 months

Materials
- Tray, teaspoon, 2 small transparent jars with labels removed, bowls or teacups
- Variety of dried beans: navy beans, lentils, black-eyed peas, kidney beans, lima beans

Spooning beans from one container to another can challenge *anyone's* coordination skills. It is especially challenging when you are two and one-half, going on three. It can also be fun if you are spooning the beans for a purpose — to make a colorful jar of layered beans for the family to look at and admire. Because young children so often use beans to explore body openings, supervise this activity closely.

Your toddler may want to transfer beans from one cup to another.

Before starting, put together a model for your child to refer to. Spoon a layer of each kind of bean into one of the jars until it is full.

Show your child the jar and invite her to make one, too. Place each type of bean in a plastic teacup or bowl. Place the jar on the right side of the tray if she is right-handed, and on the left side if she is left-handed. Put the spoon in the middle of the tray and the dishes of beans on the table along the top of the tray.

Explain the activity to your toddler: **"Let's put the beans in layers in the jar."** She may not know the meaning of the word *layer*, but as you use the word during the activity she'll begin to understand its meaning. **"Which type of beans would you like to put in the jar first? Do you want to begin with the lima beans?"** Put the cup of lima beans to the side of the jar. **"Pick up some lima beans with the spoon and put them into the jar."** Encourage her to spoon the beans until the bottom of the jar is covered. Then ask if she would like to put a different type of bean in the jar. Encourage her to put at least one layer of each type of bean in the jar. When the jar is full of beans, screw on the lid. Then display the jar someplace where the whole family can see it and compliment her on the good job she did.

Keep in mind that your toddler may want to spoon her own way. The idea of layers of beans may not be as appealing to her as it is to you. Be sure to respect her opinion.

Look for other opportunities for your child to practice transporting things on a spoon. She may serve herself vegetables and rice at mealtime. Or she may be able to help out in the kitchen by spooning beans, rice, sugar, flour, or noodles from a measuring cup into a bowl or pot. 🏃

15. HOW MANY?

Age Range
30-36 months

Materials
• Groceries or kitchen utensils

Your child is becoming aware of the world of numbers. He may already recognize *one* or *two* objects without counting when you ask, "How many?" When he helps you in the kitchen, there are many opportunities for you to ask that question. Help him count one, two, or three objects in response.

When your child helps you put groceries away, count them with him:

- **"Here's one box of rice. How many? Say 'One.'"**

- **"Put these melons on the table. How many are there? One, two, three. How many? Three. Right, three melons."**

When he is setting the table, hand your child one, two, or three items at a time: **"Here are some spoons. How many are there? Yes, two. Put them on the table, please."**

When your child helps you clear the table, play a simple counting game. Ask for a specific number of things at a time: **"Put one bowl in the sink. Now put three spoons in the sink. One, two, three. Put these three spoons in the sink."**

Use other everyday opportunities to help your toddler count objects: **"Put three ice cubes in each glass, like this — one, two, three ice cubes. How many ice cubes are in the glass? Yes, three."**

16. NAMING THE DIFFERENT ONE

Age Range
30-36 months

Materials
• Silverware and dishware

By adding a few extra minutes to the job of putting away the dishes, you can also add two new words to your child's vocabulary — *same* and *different*. The following activity can be done while emptying the dishwasher or drying the dishes. It will help her learn to evaluate, think logically, and to discriminate among the things she sees.

Invite your child into the kitchen to play a game and to help you put away dishes. Pick up three spoons and a fork. Show her one spoon and ask her what it is. Put the spoon in your other hand. Pick up a second spoon and again ask her what it is. Put the spoon in your other hand and repeat the procedure with the third spoon. Then hold up a fork and ask her to name it. Point to each piece of silverware you are holding and name it: **"Spoon, spoon, spoon, fork. This is a spoon. This is a spoon. This is a spoon. They are all the** *same.*" Then point to the fork: **"Is this a spoon? No, it's** *different.* **It is a fork. Which one is different? Yes, the fork is different. Take the one that is different. That's right. The fork is different. Will you put the fork away for me?"** Help your toddler put the fork away if she can't reach the drawer. You can also put the spoons away at the same time.

Do the activity again, using different combinations of silverware. You can also use dishware by placing three identical bowls and a plate on the counter. Use the same procedure you used for the spoons and the fork. Once your child has caught on to the idea of *different*, simply show her three identical and one different item and ask, **"Which one is different?"**

Take advantage of other opportunities to teach your toddler the meaning of *same* and *different*. At mealtime show her three apple slices and an orange slice and ask which one is different. When folding clothes, put three identical undershirts and a sock in front of her. Ask her to point to the one that is different. When you are outside, pick three dandelions and a daisy. Then ask her to tell you which flower is different.

17. MAKING A MEAL

Age Range
30-36 months

Materials
• See below

Creating in the kitchen is usually a rewarding experience. Your child will not only enjoy how his creation looks and smells, but also how it tastes. The rewards are likely to be even greater when he makes a whole meal to share with you and others.

Since your child is preparing most of the meal, each dish is simple to make. The main course includes Pigs in Blankets (hot dogs wrapped in crescent rolls) and Relish Kabobs, and is followed by Fruit Salad for dessert. A glass of milk will complete the meal. Following are the recipes in the order in which they should be prepared. For each recipe, explain to your child what he needs to do and show him how to do it. If he seems to understand, let him do the work by himself while you watch. Be sure that he washes his hands before you begin.

Fruit Salad (1 serving)
    Lettuce
    Banana (3 slices)
    1/4 cup finely chopped peanuts
    Apple (3 slices)
    Maraschino cherries
    Mandarin oranges

Making gelatin.

• Show your child how to cut the banana into slices using a table knife. They will vary greatly in size unless you make a knife mark at each place he should slice. Three slices are needed for each salad.

• Place the peanuts in a bowl and show your child how to roll the banana slices in the peanuts.

• While he is preparing the bananas, drain the oranges and put them in a bowl. Slice an apple, and put some maraschino cherries into a bowl. Tear off one leaf of lettuce for each salad you are making. (You may want to prepare some of these things before involving your child.)

• To put the salad together, ask your toddler to put a leaf of lettuce on a plate. On the lettuce help him put three banana slices (count with your child), three apple slices, and 1/4 cup mandarin oranges. Let him sprinkle several cherries on top.

Pigs in Blankets
Hot dogs
Tube of crescent-roll dough (found in refrigerator section of grocery store)

- Remove one square of dough and lay it in front of your child so one corner is facing him.

- Show him how to place a hot dog on the corner of the dough and roll the hot dog so the dough wraps around it. Pinch the corner and edge of the rectangle into the dough to seal it.

- Show your child how to place the rolled hot dogs on an ungreased cookie sheet. Put the cookie sheet in the oven yourself and bake at 450° for 15 minutes.

Relish Kabobs
Soft bread cut into small squares
Pitted olives
Sliced pickled beets (cut in fourths)
Uncooked mushrooms
Lettuce leaf
Green pepper squares
Yellow squash slices
Toothpicks

- Place the lettuce leaf on a plate and put all of the other items in a bowl.

- Invite your child to select three items and to put them on a toothpick. Show him how to slide the first item down the toothpick to make room for the others. Encourage him to make other kabobs using different combinations each time.

18. IDENTIFYING FOODS BY TASTE

Age Range
30-36 months

Materials
- Breakfast or lunch foods

Most children love guessing games and most love to eat. This activity combines eating and guessing, so it is bound to be a hit with your child. In addition to adding a new twist to her meal, the activity will help her learn to evaluate and to distinguish tastes.

To make sure your child doesn't see you preparing her meal, interest her in a favorite activity outside the kitchen. If she is curious about what's for lunch, explain that you are going to play a special game at lunchtime so she must stay out of the kitchen. Once the meal is ready, seat your child at the table and say, **"We are going to play a special game today. I want you to guess what you are having for lunch. Cover your eyes with your hands. Then I'll give you a bite of something on your plate and you tell me what it is. It isn't fair to look at the food. I want you to tell me what it is just by tasting it."**

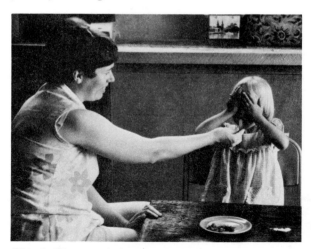
If it tastes like an apple, it must be an apple.

Give your toddler a taste of each thing on her plate. Ask her to name each food after tasting it. After she has identified every item, let her finish her mystery meal with open eyes. On another day have her cover her eyes and then ask her to guess what's for lunch by smelling the food.

Chore-time Chums

1. Naming Objects
2. Putting Away Toys
3. Dressing Up
4. Matching Toys to Their Pictures
5. Hammering
6. Following Directions
7. Opening and Closing
8. Sweeping, Vacuuming, Shoveling
9. Sponging
10. Doing Laundry
11. Hanging Up Clothes
12. Stringing
13. Washing the Car
14. Washing Windows
15. Sorting Colors
16. Folding
17. Washing Tables

1. NAMING OBJECTS

Age Range
18-24 months

Materials
• Dustcloth

Your toddler may be using single words to talk to you, or he* may be saying simple sentences. Language development differs greatly from one child to another, so don't panic if your toddler isn't spouting phrases like the two-year-old down the street. Although he will speak at his own rate, he does need to hear you talk so that he knows how to do it. He also needs friendly encouragement from you so that he will feel free to try some talking. So talk to him, listen, and praise every effort he makes to speak.

As you work around the house, encourage your child to name objects when he uses them. For example, if he points to a toy that he wants, ask him to say the name of that toy before you give it to him: **"Do you want this car? Tell me what you want. Say 'Car.'"**

When you want to dust furniture, ask your toddler to give you a hand. Give him his own dustcloth and ask him to dust with you. As you both work, name whatever piece of furniture he is working on and ask him to repeat the label: **"You're dusting the table, (child's name). Say 'Table.'"** Praise any efforts he makes to say the name of the object: **"Yes, that's the table. Good try!"**

Once your child realizes that you want him to name the objects, ask him to label them without telling him the name first: **"What are you cleaning now? What is that?"** If he doesn't say anything, tell him the name of the object and ask him to say it. If he goes

*In odd-numbered activities, the toddler is referred to as a boy. In even-numbered activities, the toddler is referred to as a girl.

Toddlers have a way of turning chores into games.

back to redust something, ask him to name it again. By the end of the cleaning session, he may have learned a few new words.

2. PUTTING AWAY TOYS

Age Range
18-24 months

Materials
• Container or storage area for toys

Sharing the household with a toddler can be messy. How many times have you stepped on a toy, shared your bath with a toy, or picked up toys and put them away? Clutter and toddlers go together — but there are some things you can do to help the situation.

Arrange a particular room or part of a room as a play area. It can be your child's bedroom, a family room, the basement, a corner of your living room, or an outdoor area if the weather is nice. Let your child know that this is the special place where she can keep her* toys and play with them.

Set up a specific storage area. It might be a set of shelves low enough for your child to reach, a toy box, a large carton, or a cabinet that she can open herself. Make sure that she knows where the storage area is and show her how to put the toys in it. (She'll discover how to take them out by herself.)

Praise your child lavishly for putting away her toys: **"Put your puzzle in the box, (child's name). Good job!"** As far as she is concerned, there isn't enough praise in the world for doing this task! 🏃

3. DRESSING UP

Age Range
18-24 months

Materials
• Adult clothes
• Zippered suitcase

When you need an absorbing task to keep your toddler busy while you work, try this one. Dress-up is a game that will surely delight him and keep him involved for a while. He will especially enjoy wearing a mommy or daddy costume that you put in a suitcase for him. If you pack a small case that zips to close, he can take the clothes out and put them back in by himself.

Hats, shoes, gloves, sunglasses, wigs, and purses are especially good items for dress-up, since your toddler can put these clothes on himself. Put the clothes in the suitcase. Then invite him to open it and see what's inside. He probably won't need any prompting to dress himself in the clothes.

Dressing up in shoes 'n' hats!

Stop your work to admire your child in his costume and look in a mirror together: **"You look just like a big person in that hat. Are you going on a trip with your suitcase?"** If he is enjoying the dress-up game, offer him a chair. Invite him to board the "train" or "bus" with his traveling case. 🏃

---

*In even-numbered activities, the toddler is referred to as a girl. In odd-numbered activities, the toddler is referred to as a boy.

4. MATCHING TOYS TO THEIR PICTURES

Age Range
18-24 months

Materials
- Selection of toys
- Pictures or drawings of those toys
- Tape

As you clean up, play a game of match-up. It will take a while for you to prepare this activity, but you can use the materials for months to come. And your toddler will be learning identification and matching skills, both of which contribute to cognitive development.

First choose a spot to store a selection of your child's toys. You might arrange them on a bookshelf or low shelves in a closet, or in a chest of drawers or plastic stacking containers. When you have found a spot for the toys, draw or find a picture of each

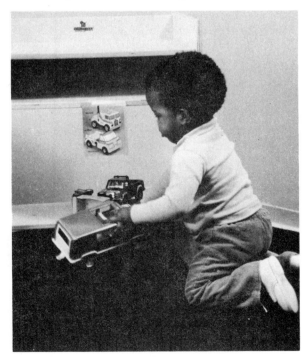

Try taping a picture of a toy to a storage area — your toddler will know exactly where to put that toy.

one. You might cut out catalog pictures, newspaper ads, or pictures from the boxes they came in. Then tape each picture to the shelf or container that the toy is stored in.

Show the toy area to your child, pointing to one toy and saying its name. Then point to the picture of that toy and say the name again. Ask her to say the name, too: **"Look at the car, (child's name). And here's a car picture. You say it: 'Car.'"**

Next, remove several toys. Hold up one toy and ask your toddler to name it. Then put that toy next to its picture. Hand her another toy and tell her to put it where it belongs. If she has trouble, show her the picture of that toy and say, **"Here's the doll picture. Put your doll here."** Continue with the other toys.

Whenever your child puts these toys away, encourage her to place them next to their pictures. When you add new toys to her collection, post their pictures, too, and show her where to put them. She will especially enjoy this match-up game if she goes through the "neat and orderly" stage that many toddlers experience.

5. HAMMERING

Age Range
18-24 months

Materials
- Piece of softwood, empty spools of thread, nails that are longer than the spools
- Lightweight hammer

Carpentry tools intrigue most youngsters. Even if you aren't handy with tools, you probably have some basic ones in your household — a hammer, a screwdriver, and maybe a pair of pliers. If you or another family member has a carpentry chore to do, your toddler would love to lend a hand. So set up his own hammering project nearby, and work side by side on your tasks.

To set up your child's carpentry project, attach the spools to the wood by placing the nails through the spools' holes and hammering them partway into the board.

Demonstrate to your child how to hit the nails with a hammer. Let him get the feel of the hammer and hit the nails — he may not pound them in, but he'll probably enjoy trying. Remember to stop and admire his work from time to time: **"You pound so hard with your hammer. Good work!"**

Clean up the materials immediately after finishing the activity. Never leave your toddler alone with these tools.

6. FOLLOWING DIRECTIONS

Age Range
18-24 months

Materials
• Laundry, dustcloth, dustpan, vacuum

Chances are, your toddler loves to "help" you do chores around the house. But does she make the job harder for you by plunging in and doing her own version of a chore? You can help her become a real chore-time chum by giving her simple two-step directions while you work together.

Whatever household job you are doing, break down part of it into two steps that your child can do. For example, if you are going to do laundry, she might take the clothes out of the hamper and put them into a laundry basket. Demonstrate for her and give the two-step directions in simple language: **"Do you want to help me?**

Okay. Please take the clothes out of this hamper and put them into the basket. Thank you! We're working together."

Your toddler can help you do part of many household jobs such as putting groceries away, folding laundry, holding a dustpan for you to sweep into, vacuuming, straightening a room, and dusting furniture.

"Please pick up the box of cereal and give it to me."

Once she is used to following your directions after you demonstrate, try giving a two-step direction without demonstrating:

• **"Please take your dish off the table and put it in the sink."**
• **"Please take these clothes into the bathroom and put them in the hamper."**
• **"Please pick up the dustcloth and dust this table."**

7. OPENING AND CLOSING

Age Range
24-30 months

Materials
- Laundry to be put away

Your toddler learns *opposites* by experiencing them: *hot/cold, big/little, on/off, in/out, wet/dry, happy/sad.* He will learn *open* and *close* the same way. Putting away clean laundry can be a time for teaching him these two concepts, and he'll enjoy being your helper.

When you put clean clothes into drawers and closets, ask for your child's help. Use the words *open* and *close* as much as possible when you talk to him. **"Open the drawer so we can put the socks in it. Okay, now close the drawer. Now we need to open the closet door. Can you open it by yourself?"** If he doesn't understand your directions, show him what to do: **"Watch me open the drawer. Now I'll close the drawer. Open it. Close it. Now you open the drawer. In go the socks. Close the drawer. Thanks for your help!"**

As you go from room to room, you might also practice whenever you come to a door: **"We're finished in this bedroom. Close the door. Oh, I forgot something. Open the door again, please."** 🧒

8. SWEEPING, VACUUMING, SHOVELING

Age Range
24-30 months

Materials
- Child-size broom and regular broom, dustpan
- Vacuum cleaner
- Toy snow shovel and regular snow shovel

Household chores that may seem dull and routine to you are challenging and new for your young child. She has seen you sweeping floors and vacuuming rugs and perhaps shoveling snow off sidewalks. Because you do these jobs, she would love to try them, too. She will experience the challenge of manipulating large tools.

Sweeping floors. Stand behind your child and help her sweep the child-size broom back and forth. When she can do it alone, grab another broom and sweep together. Then show her how to hold a dustpan while you sweep the dirt into it. This probably won't be the neatest sweeping job you've ever done, but it won't be the dullest either.

Vacuuming rugs. Your toddler is probably well aware of the vacuum cleaner. It's noisy, and you can move it around, and it even makes things disappear! Let her move the hose of the vacuum cleaner over a carpeted area. Lend a hand if the hose is too heavy for her. Never leave your toddler alone with the vacuum cleaner — she might hold the sucking hose to her ear or other body parts and hurt herself seriously.

Shoveling snow. This job is always easier with a helper! Give your child a toy shovel and show her where to dump the shoveled snow. Don't be surprised if she gets sidetracked on the job and uses her shovel for digging holes in the snow. 🧒

9. SPONGING

Age Range
24-30 months

Materials
- Unbreakable bowl or bucket
- Sponges

Using a sponge can be a very grown-up thing to do, and it requires good eye-hand coordination. So when you are cleaning the bathroom, assign the tub to your toddler. He can get right in and wash without creating too huge a mess. You might even take his clothes off before he begins and dress him again after the job is done. Or use this activity just before bathtime.

Toddlers like to think up their own sponging tasks.

Fill a bowl with water, put a sponge in it, and place the bowl in the empty bathtub. Do not use any toxic or vapor-producing cleaning products. After your toddler is in the tub, show him how to squeeze the water out of the sponge. Put the sponge back in the bowl and let him squeeze the water out a few times. Then demonstrate how to wipe the tub with the sponge — using both long strokes and short ones. As you clean the rest of the bathroom, let him concentrate on his job. Admire his good cleaning from time to time.

If your child tires of his job before you finish cleaning, set up another sponging activity. Put an empty bowl next to the one filled with water. Show him how to dip the sponge into the water and then squeeze the water into the empty bowl. Ask him to transfer all the water from the full bowl to the empty one. If he enjoys this task, you will have plenty of time to work on the rest of the bathroom.

10. DOING LAUNDRY

Age Range
24-30 months

Materials
- Sturdy chair
- Laundry to be washed

If your toddler likes gadgets, she will love to help you prepare the washing machine for a load of laundry. Simply put a sturdy chair next to the machine for her to stand on. Then put the basket of dirty clothes within her reach.

Ask your child to put the dirty clothes into the washing machine. Stand nearby and name the items as she drops them in: **"In goes a shirt. Now what are you putting in? Yes, it's a sock. Oh, here's another dirty shirt. Put that in, too. What else is there?"** Your questions can arouse her curiosity.

Measure the detergent and show your child where to pour it. Then show her where to set the dial or tell her which buttons to push in order to turn on the machine. She will feel very grown up when she turns on the big washing machine by herself!

Your child may want to help you take down the wash.

Make sure that you remove the chair when your child is finished, and warn her never to play with the washing machine unless you are there. In addition, make sure that she cannot get into detergents, bleaches, spot removers, and other laundry hazards. A locked laundry area is the safest laundry area. ✖✖

11. HANGING UP CLOTHES

Age Range
24-30 months

Materials
• Clothing hooks or a coat tree
• Paper, crayons, tape

You will be surprised at what a help it can be when your toddler hangs up his own clothes. Although he doesn't have the coordination to put his things on a hanger,

he can hang them from a hook that is low enough for him to reach. Find a spot in his room or in a closet where you can install some hooks at his level. You might also purchase or build a child's coat tree.

Show your child his special hooks and explain that this is where he can hang his clothes: **"These are your very own hooks. You can hang your clothes here all by**

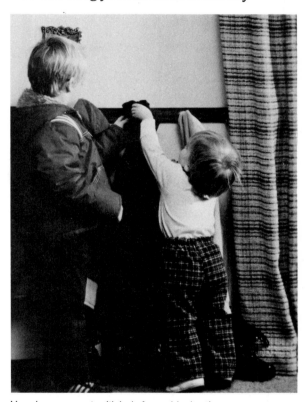

Hanging up a coat, with help from older brother.

yourself." For identification (and decoration), draw pictures of his coat, hat, pants, shirt, and other clothing items and tape them above the hooks. Show him how to hang clothes from the hooks. If he needs assistance, stand behind him and help him hang some things. Then encourage him to do it alone.

Whenever your child takes off his outdoor clothes or undresses for bed, remind him to hang the things on his hooks. Try to be consistent. Habits are formed early, so now is the time to encourage him to take responsibility for himself. And when he does, be sure to praise him. ✖

wear it as a necklace. Store the stringing materials near your sewing things and take them out for her to use whenever you sew. ✖

12. STRINGING

Age Range
24-30 months

Materials
- Shoelace
- Empty spools, macaroni, washers, giant paper clips, measuring spoons, and other "stringable" items (all larger than 1" diameter)

When you have mending or sewing to do, your toddler may want to give you a hand. Reward her interest by setting up a stringing project for her to work on while you sew. This way the two of you can work side by side. With a two-year-old's imagination, she may pretend she is sewing just like you while she strings things together.

Tie a large knot in one end of the shoelace and ask your child to watch as you string one of the objects. Then invite her to string an object. Talk about what she is doing and help her if she needs a hand: **"First, poke the string through the hole. Now pull the spool along the string. Look, the spool is hanging on the string! Do another one!"**

Encourage your toddler to work by herself while you sew. Praise her work from time to time, and show her your own project. When you are both finished, tie the ends of the shoelace together and invite her to

13. WASHING THE CAR

Age Range
30-36 months

Materials
- Old clothes for child
- Sponges, bucket, hose

Washing the car can be fun for two or more family members to do together. Your young child will practice working cooperatively with others and sharing materials with them. You can also help him increase his vocabulary while you do this job.

Your toddler will probably be wet by the end of this activity, so dress him in old clothing and choose a warm day. Show him how to dip a sponge into the water and wipe it across the car. Name each part of the car for him as you're washing: **"The wheels of the car are dirty. Let's wash the wheels. Now we are washing the bumpers. Wash the headlights, too."**

When it is time to rinse the car, let your child use the hose. Ask him to rinse off car parts that you name: **"Rinse the hood; now the doors. Can you rinse the tires?"**

14. WASHING WINDOWS

Age Range
30-36 months

Materials
- Paper towels or cloth rags

Your child probably enjoys helping you with several routine chores. For her, housework is intriguing play — especially because she sees you doing it. When you need to wash windows or patio doors, let your child lend a hand. Remember that it will take a little longer when you have your young helper, so schedule some extra time for the job.

Give your child a damp paper towel or rag for her window washing. You can wash from the outside of the house while she wipes the window from the inside. She will think it is hysterically funny if you make a few silly faces through the window before you begin.

To make the job extra fun, ask her to hold her rag on the glass. Then hold your rag over hers from your own side of the window. Tell her to move her rag around the glass. As she moves hers, try to follow it with yours. Once she catches on, ask her to follow your rag while you move it: **"Now I'll move my rag on the glass. Catch my rag with your rag."**

15. SORTING COLORS

Age Range
30-36 months

Materials
- Laundry to be sorted

Learning colors is not an easy task for a 2 1/2-year-old. He'll need to hear the names of colors many times before he begins to understand what red, blue, and yellow are. One way to help him learn the names of colors is by sorting clothing in the following manner.

While separating dark clothes from light clothes, give your child a pile to sort. Place two colors of clothing in the pile; select a light color and a dark color. You probably won't have any trouble finding four or five pieces of white clothing. If you have several navy blue, black, or red things in the laundry basket, use one of those colors.

When selecting a color, stick to articles of clothing that are the same shade. If you are using white and blue clothing, don't use both light and dark shades of blue.

Toddlers enjoy sorting toys, too.

Ask your toddler to sit on the floor in front of the pile of clothing. Explain, **"When I do laundry, I wash all the light things together and all the dark things together, so I have to sort the laundry before I put it in the washing machine. I have a pile of clothes to sort, and I made a pile for you to sort."** Pick up something white from the pile. **"This sock is white. Can you find something else that is white? Yes, the washcloth is white. Since the sock and washcloth are both white, let's put them in a pile together."** Place the two items in a pile to the left of him. Continue, **"This sock is blue. Can you find something else that is blue? That's right, the jeans are blue. We'll put them together over here."** Place the items on your child's right. Go on to ask him to pick up something and place it with the white things if it is white or with the blue things if it is blue.

If your toddler puts something in the wrong pile, help him correct his mistake: **"All of these things are white, but this shirt is blue. Put the blue shirt over here with the other blue things."** When he is finished, put his two piles in with the piles you are sorting (explain what you're doing) and give him a pile of two different colors to sort.

16. FOLDING

Age Range
30-36 months

Materials
• Laundry to be folded

Whether this is your first, third, or fifth child, the amount of laundry you do each week is greatly increased from pre-child days. Since it is something you do often, laundry work is a good activity for your toddler. To involve her, show her how to help you fold washcloths, handkerchiefs, small towels, or cloth napkins. The procedure for folding each is the same.

When folding laundry, invite your child to help you: **"I have a lot of laundry to fold. Would you please help me? I know you can do it, and it would make me feel very happy if you helped. Your job can be folding the washcloths. Watch while I show you how to do it."** Lay the cloth in front of you. Take hold of the bottom corners and place them on top of the top corners. Run your fingers along the fold at the bottom. Turn the cloth clockwise so the fold is on the left side. Take the bottom two corners and bring them up to meet the top edge. Run your fingers along the bottom fold.

"Now let's fold a washcloth together." Point out the bottom corners to your toddler: **"These are the corners of the washcloth. Hold the corners as I'm doing. Bring the corners up to these corners. Press your fingers along the fold so it will be smooth. Now turn the cloth. Hold the**

Folding a washcloth can be a difficult task for a toddler.

corners at the bottom and bring them up to the top corners. Smooth out the fold with your fingers. You did a good job. The washcloth looks great!"

You may have to fold a few more washcloths with her before she gets the hang of it. Help her only when she needs it and give her lots of encouragement as she is learning and after she is folding on her own. You will probably have a willing helper running to your side each time she sees you with a basket of clean clothes.

17. WASHING TABLES

Age Range
30-36 months

Materials
- Low, washable table or counter
- 2 unbreakable bowls, sponge, dish towels, liquid detergent, spoon

There are few things more appealing to toddlers than a bucket of soapy water. You can put that interest to good use by teaching your child how to wash a table. He's bound to enjoy learning this new and useful skill. By learning to wash the table

from left to right, he'll also be learning some prereading and writing skills. As a bonus, you'll get a sparkling clean table.

In order for this activity to be a success, you need to be well prepared. Fill the two bowls half full of water and have the sponge, towels, and detergent at hand.

Explain what you'd like your child to do: **"This table needs to be washed. It would be a big help if you would wash the table while I sweep the kitchen floor. I think I have everything you need — soap, two buckets of water, a sponge, and a dish towel. Watch while I show you what to do. First we need to put some soap in one of the buckets. Would you squeeze some soap in? One squeeze will be enough."** Demonstrate the remaining table washing steps to your child.

- Place an object in the upper left-hand corner of the table to remind your child where to begin. **"Whenever you wash the table, always begin here, by the spoon."** Place the sponge in the soapy water and squeeze out the excess water. Begin by the marker, moving across the table in a circular motion. When you get to the end of the table, dip the sponge in the soapy water and squeeze out the excess. Move across the table again, starting at the left-hand side. Repeat this procedure until the entire tabletop has been cleaned.

- Dip the sponge in the clear water and squeeze it dry. Move from left to right as you wipe off the soapy water. When you reach the end of the table rinse out the sponge and begin again on the left-hand side. Continue until the whole table has been rinsed.

- Dry the table using the dish towel. Move across the table the same way you did for rinsing.

There is a good chance your child won't sit still for the entire demonstration. Let him try each step after you have demonstrated it — you wash, then he washes; you rinse, then he rinses, and so forth. He might not want to wash the whole table before going on to rinsing. Encourage him to complete one step before going on to the next. Sticking to a job from start to finish is a good lesson to learn.

Give your child as much help as he needs. You may need to guide his hand a time or two or demonstrate some of the steps again. After a little practice, he will be able to wash the table by himself while you do another household chore.

Washing in a left-to-right movement.

Bathtime Business

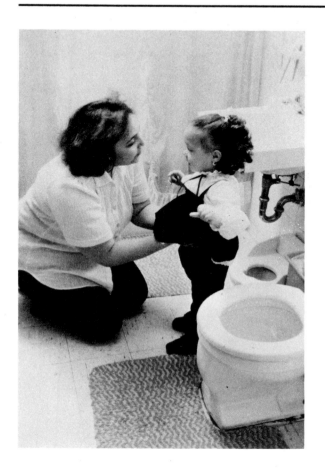

1. Ins and Outs
2. Wearing a Clown Face
3. Bathtime Puppet
4. My and Your
5. Pouring Water into a Container
6. Bathtime Pantomime
7. Counting
8. Using a Washcloth
9. Choosing an Object
10. Blowing Bubbles Under Water
11. Splashing Fast and Slow
12. Identifying the Missing Object
13. Float or Sink
14. Making Bubbles
15. Playing with Boats
16. Swimming Practice
17. Identifying Items in Partial View
18. Sorting Little and Big

1. INS AND OUTS

Age Range
18-24 months

Materials
• Plastic doll or animal

Your toddler may already understand a few pairs of opposites, such as *big/little, up/down,* and *hot/cold.* At bathtime use a plastic doll or animal to teach him* another opposite — *in/out.* Keep in mind that children learn at varying rates.

When he's in the tub, show your child the doll. Hold it on the edge of the tub and then make it step into the water. Encourage him to use the word *in* to tell what the doll is doing: **"Here comes your baby — *in* the water. You say it: 'In.'"** Then put the doll back on the edge of the tub and use the word *out:* **"Now he's *out* of the water again. Say 'Out.'"**

Let your toddler make the doll go in and out of the water and encourage him to say the words *in* and *out* as he plays. Then invite him to move the doll in or out of the

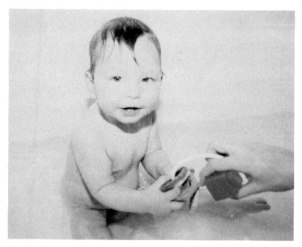

Playing "In and Out" with a shaker toy.

water on command: **"Make your doll go *in* the water. Splash! Now he wants to come *out.*"** 🧑‍🤝‍🧑

2. WEARING A CLOWN FACE

Age Range
18-24 months

Materials
• Shaving cream or cold cream
• Hand mirror

Now that your toddler is familiar with her image in a mirror, she* will enjoy making it change with makeup and costumes. At bathtime you can help her turn herself into a silly clown — with a minimum of mess.

When your child is in the tub, ask her to look at herself in the mirror: **"Look in this mirror, (child's name). Who is that? You look so clean. Show me your clean nose (ears, hair). Where's your mouth (eyes)? What a nice face!"**

Show your child the shaving cream and squirt some on her hand (or use cold cream). Tell her to put it on her chin and to look in the mirror again.

Ask if she would like to make her face look like a silly clown's face. If she resists, respect her feelings. (She might enjoy putting shaving cream on other body parts, such as arms, legs, hands, knees, and tummy.) If she does want a clown face, dab some cream on her chin, cheeks, nose, and upper lip. DO NOT PUT CREAM NEAR HER EYES. Have her look in the mirror again and share her enjoyment.

*In odd-numbered activities, the toddler is referred to as a boy. In even-numbered activities, the toddler is referred to as a girl.

*In even-numbered activities, the toddler is referred to as a girl. In odd-numbered activities, the toddler is referred to as a boy.

After the activity, put away the shaving cream or cold cream so that your toddler can't reach it. Always supervise this activity. 🧍🧍

Whenever your child does say something to the puppet, have Scrubs respond: **"Soap? Oh yes, there's my soap. Thank you for finding it."** 🧍🧍

3. BATHTIME PUPPET

Age Range
18-24 months

Materials
• Washing-mitt puppet (See *Educating on a Shoestring*)
• Soap

Puppets are a wonderful way for you and your toddler to create a world of fantasy. When you use a puppet to talk with him, that puppet becomes real in his mind. Even if your child is not a "talker," the puppet may coax some words out of him.

Introduce the puppet to your toddler: **"This is Scrubs, the puppet. He's going to wash you."** Have the puppet cozy up to your child by rubbing his arm, saying a rhyme, giving a kiss, or diving under the water. Then ask him to say hello to the puppet. Don't be surprised if he gives Scrubs a hug or kiss. He might even say more than hello.

Once your child feels comfortable with his friend, have the puppet rub himself on some soap and wash your little one's body. While Scrubs is busy, have him talk and ask simple questions that your child can answer:

• **"What part should I wash next?"**
• **"What's this sticky stuff on your face? Did you eat peanut butter?"**
• **"Where did my soap go?"**

4. MY AND YOUR

Age Range
18-24 months

Materials
• Washing-mitt puppet (see *Educating on a Shoestring*)

It will take time for your child to understand how to use the words *my* and *your*. Since the speaker and subject determine which term is to be used, your little one can confuse them easily. If you use these words often when you talk to her, she will eventually learn how to use them. Bathtime is an especially good time to introduce and review *my* and *your*.

Use Scrubs the puppet (see previous activity) to wash your child. Talk about what you are doing as you wash. Remember to emphasize the word *your*: **"Scrubs is washing *your* arms and *your* elbows. Now he's scrubbing *your* dirty hands. Show Scrubs *your* hands now. They're clean!"**

Then use Scrubs to wash your own arms, hands, and elbows and emphasize the word *my*: **"Scrubs is washing *my* hands. Now he's washing *my* wrist. Look, here's *my* clean hand!"**

Ask your toddler to show Scrubs different parts of her body. Use the word *your* often: **"Where's *your* foot? Scrubs wants to wash *your* foot now. There's *your* foot!"** Then ask her to label her body parts using the word *my*: **"Where's *your* foot? Yes, say, 'Here's my foot.' Now show Scrubs *your* leg. Say, 'Here's my leg.'"** 🧍🧍

Compare body parts when you're out of the tub, too.

Invite your child to pour the water from his cup back into yours. Put your hand over his and guide him if he needs help. He will probably use both hands to pour.

Pour back and forth for a while and then switch cups so that you have the smaller one. It will be harder for your child to pour water into the small cup. 🏃

5. POURING WATER INTO A CONTAINER

Age Range
18-24 months

Materials
- 2 plastic cups: one small, the other large

Pouring water from one container into another takes a steady hand and lots of practice, but your toddler's fascination with water will make the task seem like a game. Introduce him to pouring in the bathtub, where sloshes and spills don't matter. For bathtub pouring, fill the tub with barely an inch of water. Remind him that bath water is not for drinking.

When your child is sitting in the tub, hand him the smaller cup and let him play with it for a while. Then ask him to hold the cup steady so that you can pour into it. If necessary, help him hold the cup steady with your free hand. Then fill your cup with water and pour the water from your cup into his cup. Talk about what you are doing: **"I'm pouring water into your cup. Here it comes! Slosh, slosh. You have a full cup of water now. Mine is empty."**

On a hot summer day, try the pouring activities in a wading pool.

117

6. BATHTIME PANTOMIME

Age Range
18-24 months

Materials
- Bathroom items: hairbrush, washcloth, toothbrush, facial tissue

While your toddler is taking a bath, stage a quick pantomime. She will be delighted to show you how to use different bathroom objects that you hold up. This easy game is an introduction to the world of pretend and role playing.

After your child is washed and scrubbed, let her stay in the tub a while. Show her an object that is close at hand, such as a hairbrush. Name the object and ask her to say the name, too. Then put it down and pantomime how to use it: **"Look. I'm pretending to brush my hair with the hairbrush. You do it, too."** If she doesn't respond, she may not have understood your request. Take her hand and help her go through the pantomiming motion. Then urge her to do it alone: **"You do it. Pretend to brush your hair. That's right. Brush, brush your hair."**

Hold up other objects that are in your bathroom and ask your toddler to pretend to use them. You might show her a washcloth or towel, a toothbrush, a shaver, a facial tissue, a bar of soap, or a drinking cup.

7. COUNTING

Age Range
24-30 months

Materials
- None

Your child has many body parts just waiting to be counted. And since all of him is fully exposed at bathtime, it's a great time for counting. Right now, your child may not understand the concept of *how many,* but he will still enjoy counting along with you.

When he's in the tub or when you're drying him, point to your child's tummy and ask, **"How many tummies do you have? Let's count — one. You have one tummy."** Encourage him to touch his tummy as you count.

Point to your child's legs and count: **"How many legs do you have? One, two. You have two legs."** Ask him to point to his legs and count with you. If he needs help, hold his finger and point to each leg as you count: **"One, two. You say it, too: 'One, two.' You have two legs."**

Count other body parts together. Don't expect him to count alone, but he may surprise you. Eventually he will count on cue whenever you ask "How many?"

8. USING A WASHCLOTH

Age Range
24-30 months

Materials
- 2 washcloths
- Soap

At bathtime show your child how to use a washcloth. When she washes herself she will improve her coordination and learn about her body. But most important, she will feel proud of herself for doing a grown-up job.

Have your toddler practice washing and drying at the sink as well as in the tub.

Put your toddler in the tub and provide a washcloth for yourself and another one for her. Show her how to dip the cloth into the water and then squeeze the water out. Then rub a bar of soap on the wet cloth.

Rub the soapy cloth on your arm and invite your toddler to wash hers. Name other body parts for her to wash. When she is all lathered up, rinse out your washcloths together. Then show her how to use the washcloth to rinse the soap off her body. When she is finished, you may want to invite other family members into the bathroom to admire her big accomplishment. ✗✗

9. CHOOSING AN OBJECT

Age Range
24-30 months

Materials
• Bathroom objects: washcloth, hairbrush, toothpaste, shampoo, cotton swab

While you are watching your child in the tub, take a moment to play a short game that requires him to listen and think. All you need are several bathroom objects that he is familiar with.

Place two objects on the rim of the bathtub and ask your child to name the objects. Offer help if he needs it. Then describe one of the items and ask him to pick it up. For example, if you show him a washcloth and a hairbrush you might say, **"Show me the thing you brush your hair with."** If he seems confused, point to the washcloth and ask, **"Do you brush your hair with a washcloth? No. Do you brush your hair with a hairbrush? Yes! Now show me the one you brush your hair with."**

Remove the first two objects and repeat the procedure with two others. You might use the following descriptions:

• *Washcloth* — the one you wash with
• *Toothpaste* — what you put on your toothbrush
• *Shampoo* — what you wash your hair with
• *Cotton swab* — the thing I clean your ears with
• *Bandage* — something to put on a cut
• *Sponge* — something to wipe the sink with
• *Boat* — the thing you play with in the tub ✗✗

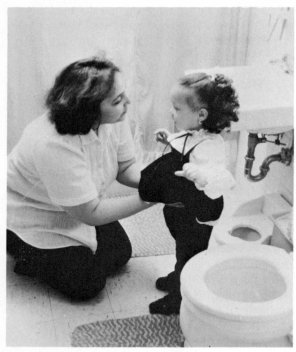

Keep in mind that toilet training is a self-help skill.

10. BLOWING BUBBLES UNDER WATER

Age Range
24-30 months

Materials
• None

As a group, two-year-olds have a very high drowning rate. There are several measures you can take to prevent such a disaster from happening to your child. Never leave her alone near a body of water — a lake, river, or neighborhood swimming pool. Even a backyard wading pool is a potential danger. So cover your toddler's own small pool when you aren't supervising; or better yet, empty it. Warn her never to go into the water unless an adult is with her. Always put a life jacket on her when she rides in a boat. And finally, help her learn to feel at ease in the water. If possible, have her take swimming lessons. (Many park districts and private pools offer lessons for infants and toddlers.)

For your small child, the big bathtub is just like an indoor swimming pool. And you can use bathtime to teach her something about breathing under water. Because it does resemble a pool, remember never to leave her alone in the bathroom.

You may need to get in the tub with your child in order to demonstrate. Tell her that you want to blow bubbles in the water with her. First, show her how to blow air out through the mouth. Hold her hand in front of your mouth while you blow so that she can feel the air. Then ask her to try it: **"You do it. Make the air come out of your mouth. Can you feel the air with your hand? Yes, you're doing it!"**

Next, invite your child to blow bubbles under water. Demonstrate first, putting only your mouth under the water: **"Look at the bubbles I'm making. You can do it, too. Just blow out air under the water. That's it! You're making bubbles."** As soon as she has mastered blowing bubbles, encourage her to put her entire face in the water while she blows. Practice blowing bubbles, coming up for a breath, and then blowing more bubbles. 🧑‍🤝‍🧑

11. SPLASHING FAST AND SLOW

Age Range
24-30 months

Materials
• None

Splashing in the tub is great fun! Unfortunately it makes a mess, and so you might discourage your toddler from doing much bath splashing. But once in a while take time to have a special splashing session just for fun. By doing so you can help your child understand the terms *fast* and *slow*. If you fill the tub with only 2-3" of water, the mess will be minimal.

When your toddler is in the tub, splash the water slowly with your hand and talk about what you are doing: **"I'm splashing the water slowly. Slow splashes. Slow."** Invite him to do it, too. **"You splash slowly. That's very, very slow. Good."** Then make fast splashes. **"My hand is moving fast now. Can you make fast splashes, too?"**

Once your child understands the terms *fast* and *slow,* ask him to splash: **"Let's see a fast splash. That's it! Now slow splashes."** Encourage him to say the words *fast* and *slow* as he splashes: **"You're splashing so fast! Say 'Fast splashes.' Now you're splashing slow. Say, 'Slow splashes, slow splashes.'"** 🏃

12. IDENTIFYING THE MISSING OBJECT

Age Range
24-30 months

Materials
- Child's tub toys and playthings
- Washcloth

Your child probably has a collection of toys that she plays with in the bathtub — toy boats, plastic animals, containers for pouring, plastic funnels, and so forth. Use some of these toys to play a game of "Take Away" with her. This is a game of concentration that requires her to look carefully and remember.

When your toddler is in the tub, place two toys in the water. While she is playing with them, point to each toy and label it. Ask her to repeat the labels. Then tell her to look at the toys while you take one away and hide it: **"Look at the toys, (child's name). Here's your boat, and here's the cup. I'm going to take away one of your toys now. See, it's disappearing."** Then ask her to tell which toy is missing: **"I took away something. What is missing?"** If she doesn't tell you,

show her the toy you removed: **"I took away the cup. Which toy is this? Yes, I took this cup away."** Repeat this procedure with other toys.

When your child can identify which toy you removed while she was watching, make the game more challenging. Show her how to cover her eyes with a washcloth. Then while her eyes are covered, remove a toy. It may take several trial runs before she catches on to this version of the game. 🏃

13. FLOAT OR SINK

Age Range
30-36 months

Materials
- Objects that float: leaf, ball of aluminum foil, acorn, plastic toy boat
- Objects that don't float: stone, spoon, penny
- Plastic bowl

The bathtub is a natural place to teach your child about things that float and things that do not float. As he plays with tub toys, he sees that they stay on top of the water. And when you drop the bar of soap, he sees that it goes straight to the bottom (unless it's Ivory). You can help him associate the words *sink* and *float* with these and other bathroom objects. All you need are some things that float and some that don't. Put these items in the bowl.

When your toddler is in the tub, say, **"Look at all these things I have for you to play with during your bath. Can you tell me their names?"** Hold up each object and ask him to name it. Put one floatable object in the water and say, **"Look, this boat stays on top of the water. It floats. Let's see which of these other things float on the water like the boat."** Pick out one thing from the bowl and put it in the water. **"Oh, look! This leaf is floating on top of the water."** Now pick out another object. **"Oops. This stone sank to the bottom. The stone does not float."** Continue until your child has placed each object in the water as you point out whether it sinks or floats.

Continue, **"Let's see if we can make the acorn sink. I'm going to push it down to the bottom of the tub. When I let go, maybe it will stay down there. Nope — here it comes! It is back on top of the water, floating."** Ask your toddler if he can make the piece of wood sink. Help him push it down and then let go. **"It popped right back up, just like the acorn."**

When you're finished, ask for some help at cleaning up. Say, **"Put the things that float into the bowl first. Good. Now put in the things that sank to the bottom. Very good. Thanks for helping me put the things away."** 🧑‍🤝‍🧑

14. MAKING BUBBLES

Age Range
30-36 months

Materials
- Large unbreakable bowl, egg beater, large spoon
- Liquid soap in plastic squeeze bottle

Bubbles are lots of fun to play with and now that your child is older, she can learn how to make them. Each step in bubble making will help her develop coordination. Remembering the sequence of steps challenges her cognitive skills.

During bathtime introduce the activity to your child: **"We are going to do something special during your bath. I'm going to show you how to make bubbles. Here is a bowl. Put some water in the bowl from the bathtub. Now I'll hold the bowl while you put in some soap."** Hand her the bottle and ask her to squeeze some soap into the bowl. Praise her for doing so and then say, **"Now you can beat up the water with the egg beater to make bubbles."** The bowl may need to go on the floor while you help your child get a correct hold on the egg beater. Describe her actions: **"Look at all the bubbles you are making. You are doing a great job turning the egg beater."** After the bowl is full of bubbles, your child may enjoy scooping them up with the spoon.

Be careful not to dump the bowl of soapy water into the tub because it is very drying to the skin and can cause urinary infections in girls. 🧑‍🤝‍🧑

15. PLAYING WITH BOATS

Age Range
30-36 months

Materials
- Toy boat
- Cargo: empty spools
- Passengers: small birthday candles
- Egg beater (optional)

Adding a boat to the bathtub may be a real treat for your child, especially if his bathtub toys are starting to lose some of their appeal. Playing with boats helps him learn what boats are used for and how they work, and it encourages make-believe. If he doesn't have a toy boat, one can be made easily (see *Educating on a Shoestring*).

Once your child is soaking in the tub, the boat can be launched. Place the boat, passengers, and cargo on the side of the tub as you say, **"It's time to launch the boat we made. Let's pretend that the side of the tub is land, the water is a lake, these candles are people, and the spools are baggage. Put one of the people in the boat and let him sail around the lake."** Show him how to push the boat through the water or how to blow it if it is a sailboat.

Some other time, stage a game of "Passengers and Cargo" in a wading pool.

You can play a number of pretend games with the boat, people, and cargo. The boat can take a passenger for a pleasure ride around the lake or it can take a passenger to the other side of the lake to visit a friend. The boat can also deliver the cargo to the other side of the lake. If you decide to make a sailboat, make two of them so you can have boat races. A calm sea can easily turn to a stormy one with the help of an egg beater. Show your toddler how to stir up the water by turning the egg beater.

At some point, turn on the faucet* and pretend it's a waterfall: **"Bring the boat near this waterfall. Will the people get wet?"** Encourage your child to think of other adventures for the boat. Ask questions to prompt him to talk about what is happening.

16. SWIMMING PRACTICE

Age Range
30-36 months

Materials
- Bathroom objects: washcloth, toothbrush, tub toys

Once your toddler is used to getting her face wet (see Activity 10 in this section), show her other water skills she can practice in the bathtub. Since the tub is a familiar, warm, and secure place, it is ideal for practicing basic swimming skills.

Kicking is fun for beginning swimmers. Draw a bath 5-6" deep and ask your child to lie on her stomach and support herself on her arms. Tell her to kick her legs when you say, "Kick, kick, kick," and to rest when you shout, "Stop!" While she kicks, encourage her to move her whole leg with

---

*Water temperature should be 120° F or lower. Either set the water heater at this temperature or install a mixing valve.

123

knees straight. Once she can kick and stop on cue, tell her to kick fast or slow on your command: **"Kick fast! Faster, faster. Now stop. Kick slowly, slowly, very slowly."**

Before using any soap in the water, you can also encourage your child to open her eyes under the water. Play a simple game to make sure her eyes are open. Hold a familiar object in front of her face when her head is under water. When she comes up, ask her what the object was. Use different objects that are handy.

Be sure to supervise this activity carefully. Never leave your child alone in the bathroom.

17. IDENTIFYING ITEMS IN PARTIAL VIEW

Age Range
30-36 months

Materials
• Bathroom objects: washcloth, soap, tub toys
• Piece of cardboard 1' square (optional)

As adults, we often identify objects when we can see only part of them. It's something we do over and over again without giving it much thought. You may see two legs around the corner and know it's your baby heading into the bathroom. You may be delighted when you see a vertical line of yellow on the bookshelf because you recognize it's the corner of the book you've been trying to find all day. Although this skill may seem very easy to you, your child probably hasn't perfected it yet. One way to help him practice identifying things in partial view is with the following bathtime game.

Position the shower curtain (or cardboard if you don't have one) so it forms a screen in front of you. Make sure your child is in full view. Announce, **"Let's play a guessing game. Watch the shower curtain. Something is going to peek out."** Hold an object behind the shower curtain and move it toward the edge of the curtain. **"Watch, here it comes."** Stop the object so he sees only part of it. **"What do you think it is?"** If he isn't sure, move it out a little further. **"Now do you know what it is? That's right! It's a cup."**

Continue playing the game using the other objects. Start by showing the most recognizable part of an object first — for example, the handle of the cup. As your toddler catches on to the task, show him less obvious parts — for example, the handle of a spoon. When he gets good at the game, hold the objects in different positions as you move them from behind the shower curtain — right side up, upside down, sideways.

As a variation, play this game after your toddler's bath, when the water is good and soapy. Keep part of an object submerged as you ask what it is.

18. SORTING LITTLE AND BIG

Age Range
30-36 months

Materials
• 2 unbreakable bowls: one small, the other large
• Objects: big spoon and little spoon, big ball and little ball, big cup and little cup
• Paper bag or box

Your child is beginning to learn that objects have characteristics that are alike and characteristics that are different. This is

what allows her to categorize items —
putting things together that have
something in common. Objects can be
categorized by shape, color, function,
texture, and size. This activity encourages
her to put big things together and little
things together. It can be done on the
living-room floor or at the kitchen table, as
well as in the tub.

Put all the objects in a paper bag or box.
Place them in the bathroom before getting
your toddler ready to take her bath.

Ask your child to sit in the tub so that she is
facing the side (and you). Announce, **"I
have a new game to play. These are all
things we will use in the game. When I
show you what's in the bag, you tell me its
name."** Hold up an object. **"What's this?
That's right, it's a ball."** Hold up the other
ball. **"What's this? Yes, it's also a ball. Here
are the balls. Take them and drop them
into the water in front of you."** Continue
this procedure until she has named all the
objects and they are in the water. (If you
have done Activity 13 in this section, you
can point out that some of the objects float
and others don't.)

Next, place the two bowls on the side of the
tub as you ask, **"What are these? Yes, they
are bowls. This is a big bowl, and this is a
little bowl."** Go on to say, **"Pick up the two
spoons. Good! Which spoon is the little
spoon? Which spoon is the big spoon?
Which bowl is the big bowl? That's right.
Put the little spoon in the little bowl. Now
put the big spoon in the big bowl. You did
it!"**

Continue until your child has placed all the
objects into the correct bowls. If she doesn't
catch on right away, she may need a little
help. Remind her of the sizes of the objects:
"This is the big spoon (point) **and this is
the big bowl** (point). **Now put the big
spoon in the big bowl! That's right. You
did it!"**

Shop, Look, and Listen

1. Turning Switches
2. Finding Foods
3. Visiting a Barbershop
4. Imitating Mechanical Sounds
5. A Song for the Car
6. Choosing Big and Little
7. Answering Yes/No Questions
8. Dressing Up
9. Identifying a Color
10. Looking Through a Magnifying Glass
11. Look and Find
12. Shape Shopping
13. Riding a Bus
14. Games for the Grocery Store
15. Where Can I Buy It?
16. Red Light, Green Light

1. TURNING SWITCHES

Age Range
18-24 months

Materials
• None

Your toddler is probably intrigued by latches and switches. If you hold him* up to a light switch, he will marvel at his ability to make the light disappear and return. When you go shopping he can manipulate a variety of knobs, buttons, and latches. Although he won't be strong enough to operate most of these switches alone, he will want to try them all with some help from you.

If your child hasn't noticed parking meters yet, give him a treat by teaching him how to operate one. First, show him which slot to push the coin into. Then put your hand over his and help him turn the switch. Generally these require some strength, so he will need your help even after he knows what to do. A word of warning — if your toddler enjoys operating meters, you may find yourself tearing him away from every one you walk past.

A water fountain is another gadget that your child will discover sooner or later. When you lift him up for a drink, let him turn the water on and off a few times by himself. Again, you will probably need to help him. (If a button operates the machine, he can do that alone.) Don't expect him to drink and switch at the same time. It requires quite a bit of coordination just to aim his mouth at the stream of running water. So after he manipulates the switch a few times, turn the water on for him while he drinks.

When you are in a store that has an elevator, let your child push the floor button. Although this task is very easy, he will love making the big machine turn on all by himself.

2. FINDING FOODS

Age Range
18-24 months

Materials
• None

Your toddler probably understands many more words than you realize. For months to come she* will be busy learning new words, but she may or may not try to say them. In either case she will store many words in her memory for the time when she wants to use them. When you are grocery shopping, take time to play a game with her that will teach her a new word or two and show you how much she already knows.

Because most produce is not prepackaged, this game is most fun to play in the produce department. When you reach that section of the store, ask your child to locate foods that you name: **"(Child's name), I'm looking for apples. Show me where the apples are."** If she is riding in the cart, she might look around and point to the foods you name. Otherwise, she can walk over to them. If she doesn't seem to understand what you are saying, offer her choices. For example, point to some oranges and ask, **"Are these the apples?"** Then point to the apples and ask again, **"Are these the apples?"** If she still seems confused, point to the correct food and say, **"Here they are. These are the apples."**

---

*In odd-numbered activities, the toddler is referred to as a boy. In even-numbered activities, the toddler is referred to as a girl.

---

*In even-numbered activities, the toddler is referred to as a girl. In odd-numbered activities, the toddler is referred to as a boy.

Identifying a bunch of bananas.

Once your child has found the food you asked for, encourage her to name it. Then ask her to put the food in your cart: **"This is an apple. Say 'Apple.' Right, apple. Now put it in our cart, like this."** Accept any attempt she makes to say the name of the food, even if it just barely resembles the word.

Try this activity in other types of stores, such as hardware stores, department stores, clothing stores, and drug stores. Keep in mind that a crowded store with many items may overwhelm and confuse your child so that she forgets words that she knows.

3. VISITING A BARBERSHOP

Age Range
18-24 months

Materials
• Doll or stuffed animal
• Hand towel

A child's first few trips to the barber can be very frightening. He will have to sit very still with a sheet fastened tightly around his neck. Then a stranger will handle his head and use sharp scissors very close to his face and ears. However, if you take a "get acquainted" trip to the barber before your child has his first haircut, he will be fascinated to watch a barber at work.

You needn't make special plans for your trip. If you happen to be near a barbershop or hair salon, stop in. The barber and customers will probably be tickled to have a young visitor.

While you watch the barber work, talk about what he or she is doing and label the tools being used: **"Those are the barber's scissors. She cuts hair with the scissors. There's the shaver. She uses it to trim very short hairs."** Although your child won't understand everything you say, he will get the general idea by listening to you and watching.

After you return home, help your toddler play "barber." Sit a doll or stuffed animal in a chair and tie a towel around its neck. Then show him how to pretend to use scissors to cut the doll's hair.

4. IMITATING MECHANICAL SOUNDS

Age Range
18-24 months

Materials
• None

Your trip to a department store with your toddler probably includes a visit to the toy department. While you look at the toys and talk about them with her, take a moment to help her focus on the sounds they make.

Find a toy that produces a sound, such as a toy instrument, a car with a siren, or a talking doll. Operate the toy so that it produces the sound and then imitate the noise: **"(Child's name), listen to this noisy top. It says *whirr-whirr.*"**

If it's okay with store employees, let your child operate the toy, too. (Some stores do not like to have children handling toys. Find out the store policy before you let your child handle toys under your supervision.) Encourage her to make the sound of the toy: *"Whirr-whirr.* **You make the sound. What does the top say?"**

Show her how to make sounds produced by other toys. Ask her to imitate their sounds without any cues from you: **"What a funny sound. What does the duck say, (child's name)? You make the duck sound."**

A busy parking lot requires parent and child to be extra safety-conscious.

5. A SONG FOR THE CAR

Age Range
18-24 months

Materials
• None

Riding in a car seat can be an exasperating experience for an active toddler. He can't move much, he can't see out the window very well, and he can't understand why you put him in the seat anyway. You can explain to him that the car seat will help keep him safe.* And you can entertain him with a song that's all about him and your visit to the store.

Before you begin singing, tell your child that you are going to sing a song about him: **"I know a song that's all about you, (child's name). And it's about the shoe store, too."** Then sing the following verse to the tune of "The Bear Went Over the Mountain."

> *We're in the car together,*
> *We're in the car together,*
> *We're in the car together,*
> *(Child's name) and I.*

If your toddler hasn't already joined in, ask him to "sing" with you as you make up other verses about your shopping trip. Although he won't be able to sing the words with you, he may hum in his own fashion or repeat one or two of the words you sing. Or he may merely kick his legs and sway his body as he listens to the tune. You might sing:

> *We'll buy some shoes together . . .*

Or:

> *We'll try to find some red shoes . . .*

As you drive along, also sing about what's happening:

> *We're stopping at the red light . . .*
> *The big white car honked at us . . .*
> *We hear the train that's coming . . .*

---

*Strap your child into a federally approved car seat *every* time he goes with you in the car. Being unrestrained in a car is the leading cause of death and injury to children after the newborn period.

6. CHOOSING BIG AND LITTLE

Age Range
24-30 months

Materials
• None

Your two-year-old is probably familiar with the words *big* and *little*. Add to her knowledge when you are grocery shopping by asking her to select items on the basis of size. She'll be giving you a hand, too.

Whenever you find an item that comes in two sizes, ask your child to select the correct size — *big* or *little*. At first, label the sizes for her and ask her to choose one. For example, **"Here's a *big* can of tuna and here's a *little* can. Please put the *big* can in our cart."** If she seems confused, name the sizes again and then show her which item to choose: **"Put this *big* can in our cart."** Remember to praise her for choosing correctly even if she needed some help: **"That's the right one! Good choice."**

Once she understands the task, ask your toddler to choose the correct size without your help: **"Can you put the *little* box of tissue in our cart?"** If there are more than two sizes to choose from, she may be confused when you ask her for the big or little item. With practice she will be able to choose the correct one easily.

For extra practice, turn to Activity 18 in *Bathtime Business*. ✖

7. ANSWERING YES/NO QUESTIONS

Age Range
24-30 months

Materials
• None

Answering yes/no questions can be more difficult for your toddler than you might realize. When you ask him a question, he must listen carefully and think about what you are saying. Then he must come to a conclusion and use the correct word to answer you. Most children learn how to answer with "no" very easily. But before your toddler is ready to answer yes, he might answer in a different way. For example, if you ask, "Do you want some raisins?" he may respond, "Raisins." Since the word *yes* is difficult to say, he may invent his own version: "ai," "es," "uh-h," or a nod of the head.

When you are shopping you will have many opportunities to practice yes/no questions with your child. While you are walking through the aisles in a store, ask yes/no questions about the things he sees:

- **"Is this a shoe?"**
- **"Do you see a clown?"**
- **"Do you want this balloon?"**

If necessary, model the correct answer: **"Is this a shoe? Yes. Is this a shoe? You say it: 'Yes.'"**

You might also ask your child questions about himself:

- **"Are you Kim?"** (child's name)
- **"Are you a boy?"**
- **"Do you have a baby sister?"**

This type of question will encourage him to become more aware of himself in relation to others. ✖

8. DRESSING UP

Age Range
24-30 months

Materials
• Dress-up kit for child (see below)

Shopping in a clothing or department store can be nerve-wracking if you have your toddler with you. Chances are, she will be bored and impatient when you are trying to find a certain item to buy. But you can help the situation by bringing along a few dress-up things she can play with.

Before you leave the house, prepare a dress-up kit to take along. You will find the kit especially helpful if you plan to shop for clothes. Fill the kit with old costume jewelry, scarves, sunglasses, caps, a brush, and a comb. When you are at the store, take out the kit if you want to look through a rack of clothes, talk to a salesperson, or try something on. To spark your child's interest in the dress up things, ask her to look at her face in a mirror. Then pull something out of the kit and put it on her: **"Look at you! You look gorgeous in that nice necklace."**

Toddlers enjoy dressing up anytime during the day.

Suggest that your toddler look through the other things in the kit while you are busy. Most toddlers enjoy dressing themselves in attractive things in front of a mirror. Keep one eye on your child and admire her costume from time to time: **"What a lovely hat! I really like those glasses on you."**

9. IDENTIFYING A COLOR

Age Range
24-30 months

Materials
• None

Identifying colors is an activity that you can play with your child as you shop. If you teach him one new color with each shopping trip, before long he will know them all.

Choose one color that your child does not already know. When you are in a store, point to things of that color and name the color: **"Here's a *green* skirt. And there's another *green* skirt. Look! The floor is *green*, too."**

Ask your toddler to say the name of the color: **"That's a *green* blouse. What color is that blouse? Say 'Green.' Right! It's green."**

As you shop around the store, ask your child to find other green things and tell you about them. Whenever you see something green, draw his attention to it. You'll find that you can do quite a bit of shopping even while helping him search for a certain color.

10. LOOKING THROUGH A MAGNIFYING GLASS

Age Range
24-30 months

Materials
• Magnifying glass

Your child is a champion investigator. Even routine shopping trips are filled with new things for her to study and learn about. It's best to establish a hands-off policy for your child in stores, but you can add to the fun of *looking* at items on display by giving her a magnifying glass. You can purchase an inexpensive magnifying glass in a dime store or the toy section of a department store. The bigger the magnifier, the better.

Demonstrate how to look through the glass and emphasize that everything looks bigger: **"Look! My finger is so big. Now your finger looks big."** While your child looks through the glass, ask her to name the things she sees: **"What do you see in there? Do you see my hand?"**

Your toddler will be more content with the magnifier if you let her ride in a shopping cart or a stroller while you shop. Hand her the things you plan to buy so that she can study them with the magnifying glass. Stop occasionally and let her look at especially attractive items on display.

Look for other opportunities to use the magnifying glass. A simple walk through the park can produce lots of fascinating items to examine.

11. LOOK AND FIND

Age Range
24-30 months

Materials
• None

Sitting in a grocery cart can be very boring for an active two-year-old. To keep your toddler content, try a special game that is just for the grocery cart. He will add some new words to his vocabulary and master the term *under*.

Seat your toddler in the child's seat of the cart. Place your first grocery items on the seat next to him so that he can reach them. When several objects are piled up on the seat, invite him to play a game of "Look and Find." Say, **"There's something hiding *under* the bread. Look and see what it is!"** If he doesn't understand, lift the bread and name the object under it. Show your surprise and enthusiasm: **"Oh! The apples are under the bread."** Then put the first item back on top of the second and say again, **"There's something hiding under the bread. Look and find it."**

Continue the game with other objects. As your cart fills up, your child will be able to reach items in the basket behind him. Whenever he lifts an object, ask him to name whatever is beneath it. If he doesn't label the object, tell him what it is and ask him to repeat the name. "It's a box of cereal! You say it: 'Cereal.'"

12. SHAPE SHOPPING

Age Range
30-36 months

Materials
• None

Your child is surrounded by different shapes, but she may not notice them and won't know their names until you point them out to her. A cracker will remain only a cracker until you show her that it is also a square. Learning the names of shapes (*circle, square, triangle*) will be one of her first math lessons.

Since stores are full of many different items, shopping time provides a good opportunity to point out shapes to your child. You are bound to find at least a few circles, squares, and triangles in each store. The first time, concentrate on circles. Whenever you see a circle, run your finger around the edge of it to outline the shape as you say, **"Look — the shape of this clock is a circle. It goes 'round and 'round."** If it can be done safely, take her finger and trace around the circle you are looking at.

After you have been on several circle-shopping trips, go on a square- or triangle-shopping trip. You don't need to plan a special trip to point out shapes, but try to remember to point them out during the normal course of your shopping. You also don't need to wait until you go shopping to point out shapes to your toddler. Your home is probably full of shapes she looks at (and eats) every day.

13. RIDING A BUS

Age Range
30-36 months

Materials
• None

As you drive to and from the store, there are probably many things to look at and talk about with your child. But driving and sightseeing are difficult (and unsafe) to do at the same time, so why not take the bus? If this is your toddler's first bus trip, the ride itself will be an exciting experience for him.

When you get to the bus stop, point out the sign and tell your child what it says: **"This sign says 'Bus Stop.' It tells people to stand here if they want to ride the bus. When the bus driver sees people standing by the sign, he or she knows they want a ride. So the bus stops to pick them up."** When you see the bus coming, explain that you need to give the driver money to ride on the bus. Give your child some change so he can pay his own fare. Let him pick out a seat, but make sure he sits near the window.

While riding the bus, talk about the things you see through the window. You might point out different stores along the way and the other kinds of vehicles on the road. Talk about how much bigger the bus is than cars and most trucks. You might also talk about where some of the other people on the bus have come from and where they might be going. Someone carrying a bag has probably been shopping and a person wearing a uniform may be going to or from work. A person carrying books may be going to school or to the library.

14. GAMES FOR THE GROCERY STORE

Age Range
30-36 months

Materials
• None

When you hear the word *shopping* you may think of plowing through crowded stores, rushing down aisles, standing in long lines, and emptying your wallet. Once in a while, plan some extra time for a grocery-shopping trip and play one of the following games with your child. You will both enjoy the shopping trip, and she will practice important visual skills.

When you have found an item you need, ask your toddler to close or cover her eyes or to turn away her head. Explain that you want to play a game with her: **"Let's play a game while we shop. For this game you need to hide your eyes. Put your hands over your eyes for a second so you can't see what I am doing."** After you have taken the item from the shelf ask your child to uncover her eyes and then show her the item: **"What is this? That's right. It is a box of cereal. Look at the shelf. Can you find a box of cereal that looks just like this one? Look for a box that has a bear on it that looks just like this bear."** Give her other clues, if she needs them, by pointing out other details to look for.

This activity may not be as easy for your child as you might think. Similar products are often packaged in a similar way. It will challenge her to look at the details of the package. If you have a lot of items to get, you may not want to play this game with each one. But occasionally ask your child to hide her eyes so you can play the game.

To overcome boredom while waiting in line, you can play another game with her. Before you both know it, it will be your turn at the check-out counter. Ask her to turn around so she can see the items in the shopping cart. (It may help if she sits sideways in the seat.) Ask her to find something that is partially in view: **"I see some cheese hiding in the cart. Can you find the cheese?"** Ask her to find other items that are partially showing.

15. WHERE CAN I BUY IT?

Age Range
30-36 months

Materials
• Pencil and sheet of paper

When preparing for a shopping trip you probably make out a list of everything you need to buy. The next time you do this, seat your child next to you. By including him in the following way, he will get practice associating items with the store in which they are purchased.

Say to your toddler, **"I have to do some shopping this afternoon. Whenever I go shopping I write down everything I need to get so I won't forget something. Will you help me make my shopping list today?"** At the top of the paper write down the type of store you will be going to (food store, toy store, hardware store, clothing store, pet store, shoe store, drug store, fabric store, book store, and so forth). Tell him, **"These are the three stores we are going to today: the food store, the clothing store, and the hardware store. I want to write down each thing I need to get at each store. I'll tell you what I need to buy and you can help by telling me where we should go to buy it."** Continue by naming specific items: **"I need to buy some milk. Do we get it at the food store, the clothing store, or the hardware store? That's right! We buy it at the food store, so I'll write 'milk' under 'Food Store.' Dad asked me to get some nails for him. Would we find nails at the food store, the clothing store, or the hardware store?**

Yes, at the hardware store, so I'll write 'nails' under 'Hardware Store.'"

Ask for your child's help as long as he's willing to give it to you. If you have 30 things to get, you obviously won't ask him to go through each one — he probably won't want to, either. Ask for his help at other times when you may be going to different stores. It is also a good game to play while riding in the car. Name an item and three types of stores. Then ask him to tell where you would find the item: **"I want to buy some fish food. Should I go to the fabric store, the pet store, or the shoe store?"**

A more elaborate game: designate shoe boxes as specific stores and then ask your toddler to put pictures of various items in the appropriate "store."

16. RED LIGHT, GREEN LIGHT

Age Range
30-36 months

Materials
• Red and green construction paper
• Popsicle stick
• Paste
• Clay

Learning that a red light means "stop" and a green light means "go" is an important lesson for your child. It will be especially useful when she is a little older and begins to venture out on her own. Meanwhile, she will enjoy knowing why you stop and go so often when riding in a car.

There are several things you can do to help your toddler understand the meaning of a red light and a green light. First she must become familiar with the color red and the color green. The most effective and enjoyable way to teach her the colors is by pointing out red items and green items throughout the day. Point out common things: lettuce, pickles, plants, and grass are green; apples, shirts, barns, and roses are red. When reading her a book, point out all the red and all the green things in the pictures.

Once your child is familiar with red and green she must learn that in traffic lights, red means "stop" and green means "go." The best way to teach her is "on location." When you are in the car on the way to a store, point out the traffic lights to her: **"See that tall pole with the light on top? It is called a traffic light. When the red light is on, it tells me to stop. See — the red light is on, so I stopped. Watch the light. It will turn green. When the light is green it means 'go.' There — it turned green, so we can go now."** Continue to point out the traffic lights during your drive. It won't be too many outings before she will know exactly what the lights mean. You can also point out traffic lights while walking with her.

On a rainy day your toddler may enjoy a game of "Stop and Go." Cut a green circle and a red circle from construction paper. When you hold up the green circle, explain that it means "go." Encourage her to move in any way she wishes. She may wiggle, jump up and down, or turn around in circles. Then hold up the red circle and explain that she should stop moving.

Your child might welcome the addition of a traffic light to her set of toy cars. Cut out a red and a green circle. Paste the circles back to back on one end of a popsicle stick. Push the other end of the stick into a lump of clay. Presto — you have a traffic light. Show her how she can use the traffic light when she plays with toy cars.

You may want to draw a complete traffic light — then play "Stop and Go" games with your child.

Teaching — Family Style

1. Kicking a Ball
2. Looking at a Family Album
3. Mirror Image
4. Follow the Leader
5. A Pretend Train
6. Rolling a Ball Through a Tunnel
7. Playing Catch
8. A Finger Play
9. Talking on the Telephone
10. Basketball
11. Repeating a Beat
12. Acting Out a Visit to the Dentist
13. Pantomiming
14. A Family Songfest
15. Family Pictures
16. Circle Dances
17. Dominoes

1. KICKING A BALL

Age Range
18-24 months

Materials
• Volleyball-size ball

Ball games encourage the members of your family to play together, and they teach young children how to take turns and play cooperatively. Try a simple game of kickball when young and old want to have some fun. Of course, before you suggest this game, make sure that your toddler can kick a ball.

Put the ball on the ground and ask your child to watch as you give it a kick. He* will probably be very willing to retrieve it for you. Then place the ball near his foot and invite him to kick it. Take turns kicking the ball until he hits it with his foot at least a few times.

To play kickball, stand with your child and tell one or two other family members to stand a few feet away, facing you. (No more than two other family members should play at a time; otherwise the game may become too rough or fast-paced for your toddler.) Put the ball down and tell your toddler to kick it to the other(s). Challenge them to kick it back while it's still rolling. When the ball heads back toward your child, ask him to grab it. Then put it down in front of him and tell him to kick it again. Let the game continue as long as everyone is having a good time.

Kick the ball!

2. LOOKING AT A FAMILY ALBUM

Age Range
18-24 months

Materials
• Family photo album

You will probably find that one of your child's favorite books is the family album. It's exciting for her* to see photographs of people and places she knows. And each picture tells a simple story about the life she is familiar with. Gather the whole family together sometime and look through the album. Your toddler can entertain everyone by identifying the people in the pictures and matching them to the people in the room.

As you flip through the album pages, ask your child to identify different people:

---

*In odd-numbered activities, the toddler is referred to as a boy. In even-numbered activities, the toddler is referred to as a girl.

*In even-numbered activities, the toddler is referred to as a girl. In odd-numbered activities, the toddler is referred to as a boy.

"Show us Grandma's picture. Is this Grandma? No, where is Grandma?" As soon as she points to the correct picture, ask her to repeat the person's name and then tell her to find the matching person: "(Child's name), where is your grandma?" Point her hand toward different family members so that she knows you are talking about people now, not pictures. "Is this Grandma? No, that's Aaron. Where's Grandma? There she is. Kiss your grandma."

Identifying family members.

Help your child describe what's happening in the pictures. Find photos that show family members in action. Use one word to describe an activity and prompt her to say it, too: "There's Mommy. She's swimming. What's Mommy doing? Swimming. You say it. Yes, Mommy's swimming." 👫

3. MIRROR IMAGE

Age Range
18-24 months

Materials
• Full-length mirror

Whenever you ask your child to identify his own body parts or to admire himself in a mirror, you are helping him learn about who he is. Different family members can look in a mirror with your toddler to help him compare himself with others. When he takes a good look at himself next to someone else, he will learn new things about his body.

First, invite your child to look in the mirror alone: "Look who's in there. What a nice looking boy!" Tell another family member to look in the mirror with your toddler. Ask them both to do something silly in the mirror: "Can you two make funny faces in the mirror? Stick out your tongues and make them wiggle."

Help them compare body parts by asking them questions: "Look — you both have wiggly tongues. Do you both have wiggly arms? Where are your wiggly feet?" Go on to give some commands: "Robert, hide behind Shuranda. I don't see Robert in the mirror anymore!" Ask other family members to look in the mirror with your toddler. If the mirror is large enough, put several people in front of it at the same time. 👫

4. FOLLOW THE LEADER

Age Range
18-24 months

Materials
• Sheets of construction paper or newspaper
• Tape

This simple version of "Follow the Leader" is a good way to introduce your child to the popular game. She will practice balance skills and learn to follow rules during a game. Older brothers or sisters, mom, dad, or others can play along with your toddler.

Make a straight path on the floor using sheets of construction paper about 12" wide. (You could fold sheets of newspaper.) Use tape to hold the paper in place. Then show the path to your toddler and the other game players. Explain, **"This is a long path you can walk on."**

Ask a family member to demonstrate how to walk on the path. After the demonstration, tell that person to stand at the beginning of the path again. This time, ask your toddler to follow the leader along the path. If she doesn't understand your request, hold her hand and guide her behind the leader. **"Here you go, (child's name), along the path."** Remind her to keep her feet on the paper as she walks along: **"Your feet are staying on the path. Good job!"**

Once your little one can stay on a straight path, extend the line of papers. Have it turn corners into and through several rooms. Invite several people in the family to join the game. Your toddler will probably want to have a turn as leader, too.

5. A PRETEND TRAIN

Age Range
18-24 months

Materials
• Kitchen chairs
• Blankets

If you have older children, they may protest when your toddler tries to join in their games. The following game can be fun for all your little ones — no matter what their ages are. If you have no other children, keep this activity in mind when other youngsters visit your home.

Use several kitchen chairs and blankets to create the train. Set up the chairs in a row, front to back. Then drape the blankets over the top of the chairs to form enclosed seats. Show the children the completed train: **"Look, here's a train for you to play in. Everyone find a seat and climb aboard."** Most of the children will enjoy sitting in the enclosed compartments. But if anyone is afraid of being under a blanket, tell him or her to sit on the blanket rather than under it.

When everyone is on the train, generate excitement with sound effects, and ask your toddler to make train sounds with you. **"*Chug, chug, chug*. The train is moving. *Toot! Toot!* Clear the track. *Choo-choo!*"** Let the children rearrange themselves and the train however they wish. The older ones will probably take over, but encourage them to include the younger tot(s) in the train play.

Playing choo-choo with friends.

143

6. ROLLING A BALL THROUGH A TUNNEL

Age Range
18-24 months

Materials
• Ball
• Towel

Playing simple games with family members is a good way for your toddler to learn how to cooperate with others. When playing a game she must follow rules, share materials, and take turns. The following game will be fun for your toddler because she won't have to spend agonizing minutes waiting for her own turn. She will also get practice rolling a ball on a specific course and catching it.

Spread the towel on the floor in a room where there is space to move. (If the weather is warm, play outdoors.) Stand in front of the towel with your legs about 3' apart. Ask your toddler to sit on the towel facing you; then tell another family member to sit behind you. Other players might stand close behind you with their legs apart to form a tunnel of legs.

Ask your toddler to roll the ball through the tunnel of legs so that the player on the other side can catch it. Then have that person roll it slowly back through the tunnel, and encourage your toddler to catch the ball. Even if she doesn't catch the ball, praise any efforts she makes: **"You almost got it. Good try!"**

As your child becomes more skilled at rolling and catching, have those forming the tunnel move their legs closer together. This will make the task more difficult. Let other family members take turns being part of the leg tunnel and playing catcher. Your toddler might also want a short turn standing with the others to form the tunnel, but don't expect her to stand still for long! ✖

7. PLAYING CATCH

Age Range
24-30 months

Materials
• Beach ball

Catching and throwing a ball is a game that most parents play with their toddlers. But until he masters the basics, this game can be very frustrating for a two-year-old. So that everyone has a good time, you and another family member might use some of the following suggestions when you teach your child how to play catch. Play outdoors or in a room with plenty of open space.

The best ball for a beginner to use is a beach ball that is slightly deflated. He can get a good grip on this type of ball and catch it easily. If your child is new to the game of catch, stand behind him and guide his hands through the first few catches and

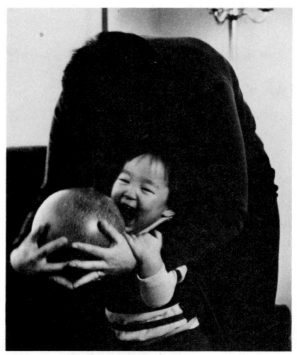

A good catch, with a little help from mom.

144

tosses. Have the other family member stand about 3' away.

Show your toddler how to hold out his arms and make a "cradle" to catch the ball in. Then have the other player toss the ball into his arms. Give him lots of praise when the ball lands in his arms: **"Good catch! You held your arms out just right."** When you help him throw the ball back to the other player, have him push the ball forward rather than throw it overhand or underhand. He can aim it more skillfully with a push.

After a few tosses and catches, let your child do it alone. Give him lots of enthusiastic encouragement and expect many mistakes. Be specific with any suggestions:

- **"Hold your arms closer together, like this. Do what I'm doing. That's right."**
- **"Watch the ball. Here it comes!"**
- **"Look at Brett. Now throw the ball to him."** ✖

8. A FINGER PLAY

Age Range
24-30 months

Materials
- None

Finger plays delight young children. You probably remember some from your own childhood that you now perform for your toddler. Teach the following finger play to other children and adults in your household so that the whole family can share it with your two-year-old.

At first, the family should say the words and do the motions for your little one to watch. But once she becomes familiar with

the rhyme, have everyone encourage her to do the hand movements.

There was a little snake.
(Place your palms together, fingers pointing forward)
She went crawling on the ground.
(Wiggle palms)
She ate lots of bugs.
(Clap palms together)
But she didn't make a sound.
(Hold forefinger to lips)
She crawled in a hole,
(Make a loose fist with one hand)
In a hole so deep,
(Poke forefinger of other hand into your fist)
That she curled up tight
(Make a ball with both hands)
And then went to sleep.
(Tilt your head to one side and close your eyes) ✖

9. TALKING ON THE TELEPHONE

Age Range
24-30 months

Materials
- Telephone

Telephones have probably fascinated your child for a long time. After all, they have many attractive features: a phone rings; voices come out of it; and it has buttons to push or a dial to turn. Best of all, your toddler has seen the whole family "play" with the telephone in your house. Now that he is beginning to use words, arrange for family members to phone him and talk.

When a family member is leaving for work or going to visit a friend, ask him or her to call home at a certain time. When that person calls, help your child hold the receiver to his ear and tell him to say hello. He may or may not respond to the speaker's words and questions. And don't be surprised if he nods or uses gestures to answer. He doesn't realize that the person can't see him!

Talking on a play telephone with grandpa.

Help your toddler initiate a conversation. For example, if you say, "Tell mama that you went swimming this morning," your child might say "Swimming." Encourage such attempts. Keep the phone call very short. After a minute or so tell your child to say good-bye and help him hang up. Be sure to tell him what a good telephone talker he is: **"You talked to mama on the phone. You told her all about our trip to the beach."**

10. BASKETBALL

Age Range
24-30 months

Materials
- Ball
- Laundry basket or wastepaper basket

A laundry basket can turn your yard into a basketball court for the youngsters in your household. One or two older children (or grown-up family members) will enjoy shooting baskets with your toddler. They can show her how to aim for the basket and can help her learn how to take turns.

Put a marker on the ground about 1 1/2' from the basket so that your toddler knows where to stand. Have a family member demonstrate how to throw the ball into the basket. Then let your toddler take a turn. Praise any efforts she makes, even if her aim is off: **"There you go. Good try!"** If she needs help controlling the ball, stand behind her and guide her arms as she throws.

Learning to take turns.

Once your child catches on, emphasize taking turns with the other players. **"Now it's Joey's turn. Let Joey have the ball. Yeah, Joey! Okay, it's your turn now**

(child's name). Make a basket!" To help your toddler wait for her turn, ask her to retrieve the ball after each player shoots. Have your older children stand farther from the basket so that they will be equally challenged by the game. 👫

11. REPEATING A BEAT

Age Range
24-30 months

Materials
• "Drums": pots and pans, boxes, books, tables

A rhythm band is a great activity for the whole family. All ages can have fun drumming and tooting, and everyone can contribute in his or her own way. In this activity make your group strictly a drummers' band. Pots and pans, empty boxes, dictionaries, encyclopedias, and tabletops can all become drums. And each drum will have its own special tone.

Let the participants become familiar with their instrument. Then ask all the drummers to stop playing and listen to you. Beat your drum one time and ask another family member to do what you did. Then beat your drum one time again and ask your toddler to do what you did. If he needs help, hold his hand and help him beat the drum one time. Let the other drummers have turns, too.

Next, tell everyone to listen very carefully and beat the drum *two* times. Let everyone have a turn to copy you. Your toddler might need several turns before he can repeat your two beats by himself. Praise him for any attempts he makes and offer lots of applause when he repeats the two beats. After everyone has had a turn, let the group finish with an impromptu jam session. 👫

12. ACTING OUT A VISIT TO THE DENTIST

Age Range
24-30 months

Materials
• Chair, plastic straws, cup of water and empty bowl, towel, large white shirt

Unfamiliar experiences can be very frightening to a young child. Visits to a dentist, doctor, barber shop, or hospital are either new or relatively new to your toddler, and so she will be unsure of what may happen. A practice session before an upcoming visit can help her feel more confident and less fearful. Include other family members in the activity by encouraging them to role-play a visit for your toddler. This activity describes ways to role-play a visit to the dentist. Adapt these suggestions to fit whatever situation your child will be in.

Create a setting for role-playing. For a dental visit, gather the materials listed above. Ask an older brother or sister or another family member to play the dentist. Tell the dentist to put on the white shirt.

Sit in the chair yourself and tell your toddler to watch carefully while the dentist checks your teeth. First have the dentist drape the towel around your neck. The dentist can use plastic straws to "clean" and "examine" your teeth. If you have a cavity, a straw can become a drill (with a few added sound effects). Once or twice, sip water from the cup and spit it into the empty bowl.

When you are finished, let your toddler take a turn in the seat. Have the dentist "examine" and "work on" her teeth. She may refuse to let the dentist work on her teeth or even look into her mouth. Don't force her. With a little persuasion she might cooperate. Afterwards, praise her for being a good patient. 👫

13. PANTOMIMING

Age Range
30-36 months

Materials
• None

You may think that charades is a game to be played by adults at parties. But all members of your family, including your toddler, can enjoy playing a simple game of charades. All you need are a little bit of space, some willing children and parents, and enthusiasm. Children enjoy acting things out and pretending. They will also get a kick out of watching mommy pretend to bounce a ball and daddy pretend to be a dog drinking.

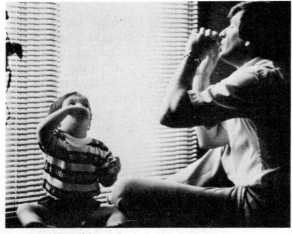
A toddler may want to pantomime along with you.

Everyone should take turns acting something out. The adults should go first, though, to explain and to show the children how the game is played. Sit together on the couch or floor, in front of the person who is pantomiming. Have that person pantomime actions that are familiar to your toddler, such as brushing hair, brushing teeth, drinking milk, licking an ice-cream cone, dialing and talking on the telephone, getting dressed, sweeping the floor, washing the face, reading a book,

running, and sleeping. Once the pantomime starts, all observers are free to shout out what they think the action is.

The person pantomiming can then choose the next person to pantomime, or you can take turns according to age (oldest to youngest), or mom or dad can pick who is to go next. When it is your toddler's turn, ask him to whisper in your ear what he would like to act out. Chances are, he won't have any ideas or will say something that has already been done. Give him a few suggestions and let him pick one that appeals to him. Be sure the rest of the family can't hear you. Ask him to show you how he is going to act it out. If he isn't sure, give him some help.

14. A FAMILY SONGFEST

Age Range
30-36 months

Materials
• Records, record player, musical instrument (optional)
• Pot lids, coffee can and wooden spoon, comb and piece of paper

Spending time together as a family is important. When your child is older, some of her earliest memories may be of special times your family had together. For parents, few things are more satisfying than having your children grow up with many happy memories of their childhood.

But it isn't easy to find activities that family members of all ages will enjoy doing together. One activity that appeals to people of all ages is singing. The baby in the family will enjoy clapping and bouncing up and down to the music. Although your toddler won't be too concerned about singing in tune, she will enjoy singing. (Hearing you sing will help her develop an ear and voice for tuneful singing.) Older members of the family will take pleasure in trying to sing in parts and watching the children sing.

Singing and clapping.

Songfests are most fun when they're spontaneous and informal. The only rule should be that everyone have a good time. Sing a variety of songs, including everyone's favorites. Three-year-olds can sing tunefully between D and G.

They need a lot of repetition to learn a song, so be sure to sing some simple songs in your toddler's range, such as "Mary Had a Little Lamb," "Twinkle, Twinkle Little Star," and "London Bridge." Sing the songs several times to help her learn the words. She'll also enjoy listening to and learning songs that you remember from your childhood — folk and country songs, religious songs, and popular songs. Try to sing a mixture of slow and lively tunes. You can sing along with records or to the accompaniment of a musical instrument if someone in your family plays one.

During the sing-alongs family members should feel free to clap, wave their arms, or dance to the music when they feel like it. Some songs may even lend themselves to a homemade band. Pot lids can become cymbals, a coffee can and a spoon can turn into a drum, and a piece of paper over a comb can sound like a harmonica.

15. FAMILY PICTURES

Age Range
30-36 months

Materials
• Roll of butcher paper, crayons, and scissors

Looking at family photo albums is an activity most children enjoy doing from the time they are quite young. The family is close to your child's heart, so it's no wonder he enjoys activities related to the family. (See Activity 2 in this section.) This activity involves drawing life-size pictures of each family member which your child can hang in his room.

Unroll a length of butcher paper on the floor (a hard surface will work best). Have each member of your family take turns lying faceup on top of the paper. Using a black crayon, trace around each one and then cut out the picture. Each family member can color his or her own figure, drawing on facial features and clothing. (Don't worry about artistic talents.) Draw on the features and clothing for your toddler. He can color in the clothing. Cut out the figures and hang them on your child's bedroom wall. He'll enjoy looking at these life-size family pictures.

16. CIRCLE DANCES

Age Range
30-36 months

Materials
• None

Your child's first dance step was probably bouncing up and down, swaying back and forth, or waving her arms. As she grew, so did her concept of dancing. She added a few new steps and maybe a turn or two. Freestyle dancing plays an important role in a child's development. It helps develop creativity, coordination, and rhythm. A dance that has specific steps to follow is also a good learning experience. It is especially fun when the whole family takes part. Three good dances to teach your child are "Hokey Pokey," "Did You Ever See a Lassie?" and "Here We Go 'Round the Mulberry Bush." They are probably dances you did as a child but which you may have forgotten.

Hokey Pokey
To do the "Hokey Pokey," everyone stands in a circle. Sing the following song, doing the actions described. If you aren't sure of the tune, it may be on a record at the library, or ask among your friends and relatives.

> *Put your **right hand** in;*
> *Take your right hand out.*
> *Put your right hand in and shake it all about.*
> *Do the hokey pokey and turn yourself around.*
> *That's what it's all about.*

Continue with: left hand, right foot, left foot, head, and whole self.

Did You Ever See a Lassie?
Everyone stands in a circle except the person leading the action. The leader stands in the center of the circle. As everyone sings the following song, the leader performs an action — waving arms, jumping up and down, turning around, clapping hands, bending up and down, shaking the head, or doing anything else he or she thinks of. Once the leader begins moving, everyone else joins in. If the leader is female, use *Lassie;* if male, use *Laddie.*

> *Did you ever see a lassie, a lassie, a lassie,*
> *Did you ever see a lassie go this way and that?*
> *Go this way and that way;*
> *Go this way and that way.*
> *Did you ever see a lassie go this way and that?*

Enjoying a circle game with friends.

The same person may lead the actions, or everyone may take turns. If everyone is taking turns, your toddler may need some help when she is in the middle of the circle. It's hard to think of an action on the spur of the moment, so ask her what she'd like to do before you sing. If she isn't sure, give her a few suggestions and ask her to choose one.

Mulberry Bush
To play this game, your family needs to stand in a circle holding hands. Walk around in a circle as you sing the following verse to the song:

Here we go 'round the mulberry bush,
Mulberry bush, mulberry bush.
Here we go 'round the mulberry bush
So early in the morning.

Stop walking and drop hands. Lead everyone in pantomime, doing a daily chore while you sing:

This is the way we (sweep the floor),
Sweep the floor, sweep the floor.
This is the way we sweep the floor,
So early in the morning.

Repeat the chorus and another verse. Change the action each time you sing the verse. You can hang up clothes, brush teeth, iron clothes, wash dishes, button a coat, comb hair, scrub floors, shake out a rug, or hammer a nail.

17. DOMINOES

Age Range
30-36 months

Materials
• Picture dominoes

Playing dominoes is an excellent way for children to practice matching. It is also a great way to spend an evening together doing something as a family. Dominoes with dots are a bit difficult for a toddler to match. Look for dominoes with pictures on them — these can be used by younger children. If you can't find picture dominoes, they are easy to make (see *Educating on a Shoestring*).

To introduce your child to the game, lay some of the dominoes faceup in front of him: **"These are called dominoes. There are nice pictures on them, aren't there?"** Hold up one of the dominoes and point to one of the pictures: **"What does this picture show? Yes, it's a dog. What picture is on the other side of the domino? That's right! It's a flower. Can you find a picture of a flower on one of the dominoes on the table?"** Give him time to look for the correct picture, giving help as needed. Praise his efforts at matching.

Go on to explain how to play this version of dominoes: **"Now listen carefully and I'll tell you how to play a game with the dominoes. First we have to turn all the dominoes over so we can't see the pictures. Now let's each take four dominoes. I'll count for you: one, two, three, four."** Continue by turning over the dominoes so you can see the pictures. Have your toddler put one of his dominoes on the table or floor. Say, **"There is a cat and a rainbow on that domino. Now it is my turn. I need to find a picture of a cat or a rainbow. Here's a rainbow, so I'll put it next to this rainbow** (point). **These are the same, so I can put them together. Now let's see what's on the ends. Here is a cat and here is a spoon. Is there a picture of a cat or a spoon on one of your dominoes? Yes, that's a spoon. Put that picture of a spoon next to this picture of a spoon."**

Continue playing the game, following the procedure described above. If a player doesn't have a domino he or she can use, draw one from the pile. If it matches, play it. If it doesn't match, it's the next person's turn.

By now you have probably realized that the rules for playing dominoes with a toddler are different from the rules you normally use — no one wins or loses. If your child loses interest in the game, that's the time to stop playing. If the game does keep his interest, it is over when all the dominoes have been played. Lots of encouragement will help to keep him enthusiastic about playing. Comment on how well he is matching and taking turns, and how long the line of dominoes is getting. ✖️

More About Small Wonder

Small Wonder is a two-level program of field-tested activities and support materials that stimulate the language development and the physical, emotional, and intellectual growth of babies and toddlers. It is used all over North America in day-care centers, preschool programs, parent-child centers, social service agency programs, home-based day care, special-education settings, pediatric centers, and homes. Level 1 is for babies from birth through 18 months; Level 2 continues with toddlers from 18 through 36 months. In addition to activity cards, each level includes a User's Guide, a puppet, picture cards, a plastic Look Book to display the picture cards, and a diary or progress chart. Level 2 also features a sound sheet containing original songs.

Small Wonder gets babies off to a good start! Delightfully inventive *Level 1* activities provide opportunities for the youngest children to strengthen muscle coordination, mimic sounds, explore their surroundings, learn to help themselves, follow simple directions, and begin to speak. Even daily routines such as bathing, diapering, dressing, and eating become special times to explore and learn when caregivers follow the clear directions given for each activity. These small wonders of accomplishment — shaking a rattle, recognizing a picture in a book, bouncing to a rhythm — are the beginning skills through which babies can learn and grow.

Lively *Level 2* activities stimulate toddlers' special readiness to speak and socialize and help satisfy children's need to start performing independently. Group games, outdoor activities, original songs, simple arts and crafts projects, and health and safety routines are presented in a fresh set of activities that give young children a sense of self-confidence and self-respect. Skills in problem solving, understanding abstract concepts, speech and language acquisition, toileting, and cooperation are some of the small wonders introduced in this new toddler program. *Level 2* follows as a developmentally sequenced continuation of *Level 1*, but it is wholly self-contained and may be used independently of the earlier program.

If you are a parent with a child in day care, find out whether your center is using *Small Wonder* and have them contact the publisher if they are not:

> AGS
> Publishers' Building
> Circle Pines, MN 55014

If you are a professional care provider, write to AGS for a free, colorful brochure on the *Small Wonder* program. In Canada, contact Psycan, Ltd., 101 Amber Street, Markham, Ontario L3R 3B2.

Editorial Reviews

"*Small Wonder* for parents and caregivers to use with infants . . . is an activity program written in ordinary language and is aimed at both caregivers and parents. Karnes has an ability to summarize the key points of development and to describe these in a manner that is immediately understandable to anyone who has ever seen an infant.

"Considering Dr. Karnes' wealth of experience, it is not surprising to find that the activities are both carefully thought out and fun for the infant and caregiver.

More About Small Wonder

"A strength of the program throughout is the extent to which it helps the adult learn about infant development.

"*Small Wonder* . . . is developmentally sound, easy to follow and to implement, and does not require fancy or expensive extras . . . If you have infants in your center, you will want to explore *Small Wonder.*"
Day Care and Early Education
Fall, 1979

"It has been a long time since I have seen material so well thought out. The pride and care in the production of the "*Small Wonder*" kit is obvious . . . it should be essential resource material in day cares, institutions for infants, parenting classes, child growth college classes and libraries. As a training guide for personnel who care for babies, it can't be beat at any price."
Southern Association on Children Under Six (SACUS)
Dimensions, April, 1980

Index of Activities According to Primary Skills Emphasized

This index lists the *Small Wonder* activities by skill category. Each category includes activities for children of different ages. Use the index to locate activities emphasizing an aspect of development you want your toddler to work on. Of course, most activities require the use of several different skills. For example, when a child works a simple puzzle, she uses visual skills to determine where a piece fits in; she uses finger and hand skills to fit each piece into place; she uses attending skills to complete the task; and she may use language skills to name the objects pictured in the puzzle. This index lists activities according to the *primary* skill emphasized in each one.

Balance and Motion Skills

18-24 Months
Climbing (#1: *On the Move*)
Walking Up Stairs (#2: *On the Move*)
Walking Backwards (#4: *On the Move*)
Walking Down Stairs (#6: *On the Move*)
Whiffle Ball (#2: *Growing with the Grass*)
Kicking a Ball (#1: *Teaching — Family Style*)
Follow the Leader (#4: *Teaching — Family Style*)
Rolling a Ball Through a Tunnel (#6: *Teaching — Family Style*)

24-30 Months
Obstacle Course (Part 1) (#7: *On the Move*)
Jumping Off a Step (#8: *On the Move*)
Somersaulting (#9: *On the Move*)
Walking the Plank (#10: *On the Move*)
Climbing Around on a Ladder (#12: *On the Move*)
Playing Catch (#7: *Teaching — Family Style*)
Basketball (#10: *Teaching — Family Style*)

30-36 Months
Obstacle Course (Part 2) (#13: *On the Move*)
Throwing On-Target (#14: *On the Move*)
Chasing Bubbles and Balloons (#16: *On the Move*)
Jungle Walk (#17: *On the Move*)
Batting a Ball (#18: *On the Move*)
Running (#18: *Growing with the Grass*)

Body Awareness

18-24 Months
Imitating Actions (#1: *Just for the Fun of It*)
Pretending to Be an Animal (#1: *Growing with the Grass*)
Wearing a Clown Face (#2: *Bathtime Business*)
Mirror Image (#3: *Teaching — Family Style*)

24-30 Months
Using Props to Act Out a Story (#10: *Just for the Fun of It*)
Whispering (#12: *Just for the Fun of It*)
Stretching (#13: *Just for the Fun of It*)
Blowing Bubbles Under Water (#10: *Bathtime Business*)
A Finger Play (#8: *Teaching — Family Style*)

30-36 Months
What's Missing? (#13: *Just for the Two of You*)
Statues (#15: *Just for the Fun of It*)
Walking Like the Animals (#15: *On the Move*)
Swimming Practice (#16: *Bathtime Business*)
Pantomiming (#13: *Teaching — Family Style*)

Cognitive Skills

18-24 Months
Playing with Sand (#3: *Growing with the Grass*)
Hide and Find in the Sand (#6: *Growing with the Grass*)
Sorting Dishes (#4: *A Classroom in the Kitchen*)
Exploring Water (#5: *A Classroom in the Kitchen*)
Turning Switches (#1: *Shop, Look, and Listen*)

24-30 Months
Working with Clay (#8: *Just for the Fun of It*)
A Nature Walk (#9: *Growing with the Grass*)
Watching the Weather (#12: *Growing with the Grass*)
Counting (#7: *Bathtime Business*)
Choosing Big and Little (#6: *Shop, Look, and Listen*)
Looking Through a Magnifying Glass (#10: *Shop, Look, and Listen*)

30-36 Months
Identifying Objects by Touch (#14: *Just for the Two of You*)
Patterning (#15: *Just for the Two of You*)
Paint-Stamping (#17: *Just for the Fun of It*)
A Walk in the Rain (#15: *Growing with the Grass*)
Planting Seeds (#17: *Growing with the Grass*)
Short and Long (#13: *A Classroom in the Kitchen*)
Naming the Different One (#16: *A Classroom in the Kitchen*)
Identifying Foods by Taste (#18: *A Classroom in the Kitchen*)
Float or Sink (#13: *Bathtime Business*)
Sorting Little and Big (#18: *Bathtime Business*)
Where Can I Buy It? (#15: *Shop, Look, and Listen*)
Red Light, Green Light (#16: *Shop, Look, and Listen*)

Index of Activities

30-36 Months
Camping Out (#13: *Growing with the Grass*)
Making a Meal (#17: *A Classroom in the Kitchen*)
Washing the Car (#13: *Chore-time Chums*)
Washing Windows (#14: *Chore-time Chums*)
Playing with Boats (#15: *Bathtime Business*)
Riding a Bus (#13: *Shop, Look, and Listen*)
Family Pictures (#15: *Teaching — Family Style*)
Circle Dances (#16: *Teaching — Family Style*)

Visual Skills

18-24 Months
Matching Objects (#3: *Just for the Fun of It*)
Matching Toys to Their Pictures (#4: *Chore-time Chums*)

24-30 Months
Lotto (#7: *Just for the Fun of It*)
Sorting (#8: *Growing with the Grass*)
Form Puzzles (#10: *A Classroom in the Kitchen*)
Identifying the Missing Object (#12: *Bathtime Business*)
Identifying a Color (#9: *Shop, Look, and Listen*)

30-36 Months
Sorting Colors (#15: *Chore-time Chums*)
Identifying Items in Partial View (#17: *Bathtime Business*)
Shape Shopping (#12: *Shop, Look, and Listen*)
Games for the Grocery Store (#14: *Shop, Look, and Listen*)
Dominoes (#17: *Teaching — Family Style*)

More Parenting Books from AGS

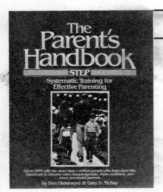